Bettendorf Public Library
Information Center
www.bettendorflibrary.com

MASTERS OF IMAGINATION

"*Maestro of collaborative mayhem*, Michael McCarty, brings brio and humor to the art of the interview with this collection of wickedly entertaining dialogues with science fiction, fantasy and horror luminaries. *Masters of Imagination* is a riveting, revealing and engaging survey of some of the major talents who shape today's genre landscape. Unputdownable!"

– J.L. Comeau, www.CountGore.com

"Michael McCarty is comparing this, his 'last' book of interviews, with that of a person perhaps writing his own obituary indeed. He has written a wonderful and lively funeral wake. After all, many of his subjects have written and showcased the undead and darker realms of existence. I predict that you, the reader, will be spellbound by this fascinating examination and exposition of the thoughts and reflections of those who have created horror and fantasy in film and the written word. In a sense, you will be reading their minds, thanks to the inquisitive and, yes, diabolical appetite of Mike McCarty what a feast you'll have!"

– The Amazing Kreskin

MASTERS OF IMAGINATION

Interviews with 21 Horror, Science Fiction and Fantasy Writers and Filmmakers

Michael McCarty

Foreword by Alan Dean Foster

Afterword by Gregory Lamberson

BearManor Media

2010

Masters of Imagination: Interviews with 21 Horror, Science Fiction and Fantasy Writers and Filmmakers

© 2010 Michael McCarty

Foreword © 2010 Alan Dean Foster
Afterword © 2010 Gregory Lamberson

All rights reserved.

For information, address:

BearManor Media
P. O. Box 71426
Albany, GA 31708

bearmanormedia.com

Published in the USA by BearManor Media

ISBN—1-59393-630-3
978-1-59393-630-3

To the Source Book Store in
downtown Davenport, Iowa.
Also to the Horror Writers Association
and the Bram Stoker Awards.

**Also by
Michael McCarty**

*Esoteria-Land: The Authentic, Eclectic and
Eccentric Nonfiction of Michael McCarty*
(Bear Manor Media, 2009)

Coming Soon:

*Modern Mythmakers: Interviews with Horror,
Science Fiction and Fantasy Writers and Filmmakers*
(Bear Manor Media, 2012)

TABLE OF CONTENTS

Acknowledgments ix
Foreword by Alan Dean Foster...................................... 1
Preface 3

I Am Dracula: C. Dean Andersson.. 9
A Real Gun-Totin', Ghost-Fightin' Heroine:
    Adrienne Barbeau.. 19
The Library Man: Ray Bradbury 25
Halloween and Beyond: John Carpenter 31
In a Dark Dream: Charles L. Grant..................................... 39
Seduced by Moonlight: Laurell K. Hamilton 45
Guardian of Lost Souls: Barry Hoffman.............................. 51
The Bone Factory: Nate Kenyon 65
Old Flames: Jack Ketchum 73
Till Death Do Us Part: Joe R. and Karen Lansdale 79
Bubba Ho-Tep: Joe R. Lansdale... 83
Puppets, Nightmares and Gothic Splendor:
    Thomas Ligotti 89
The Descent: Jeff Long... 101
A Dirty Job: Christopher Moore 109
The Night Mayor: Kim Newman 115
From *Logan's Run* to *London Bridge*: William F. Nolan.... 125
Empire of Ivory: Naomi Novik 133
The Gateway Trip: Frederik Pohl 139
Queen of the Scream Queens: Linnea Quigley 153
One-Man Movie Industry: Fred Olen Ray 163
The Jazz Man of Horror: Peter Straub............................... 171

Afterword by Gregory Lamberson...................................... 181
About the Author 183

PUBLISHING HISTORY

Previously unpublished: Christopher Moore and William F. Nolan interviews.

Previously published interviews with unpublished and updated material:

>C. Dean Andersson (2008, *Brutarian Quarterly* and unpublished material)
>Adrienne Barbeau (2003, *Horror Garage* 2003)
>Ray Bradbury (1998, *Moline Dispatch* newspapers)
>John Carpenter (2004, *Science Fiction Weekly* and unpublished material)
>Charles Grant (2002, *Hellnotes* and unpublished material)
>Laurell K. Hamilton (2003, *Science Fiction Weekly*)
>Barry Hoffman (2008, *Horror Garage* and unpublished material)
>Jack Ketchum (2010, *Brutarian Quarterly* and unpublished material)
>Nate Kenyon (2006, *Horror Garage* and unpublished material)
>Joe and Karen Lansdale (2009, *Horror Writers Association Newsletter* and unpublished material)
>Joe Lansdale (2005, *Science Fiction Weekly* and unpublished material)
>Thomas Ligotti (2008, *Science Fiction Weekly* and unpublished material)
>Jeff Long (2009, *Cemetery Dance Magazine* and unpublished material) unpublished material by Michael McCarty)
>Kim Newman (2008, *Science Fiction Weekly*: and unpublished material)
>Naomi Novik (2007, *Science Fiction Weekly* and unpublished material)
>Frederik Pohl (2001, *Science Fiction Weekly* and unpublished material)
>Linnea Quigley (2009, *Brutarian Quarterly* and unpublished material)
>Fred Olen Ray (2009, *Brutarian Quarterly* and unpublished material)
>Peter Straub (2003, *Science Fiction Weekly* and unpublished material)

Previously unpublished material:
>Forward by Alan Dean Foster
>Afterword by Gregory Lamberson

Please note: *The opinions stated by the interview subjects are not necessarily those of the author or publisher. In these candid interviews, the subjects have been allowed to speak their minds and express their personal beliefs, concerns, and views – all for the enlightenment and entertainment of you, the reader.*

Acknowledgements

First of all, I'd like to thank all the interviewees for taking time out of their very busy schedules to do the interview in the first place and providing assistance, photos and additional material for this book as needed.

Next, I really would like to thank BearManor Media and publisher Ben Ohmart for letting me publish another volume of interviews after *Esoteria-Land*. To let me continue on this journey means so much to me. I'd also like to thank the newspaper and magazine editors Scott Edelman, James J.J. Wilson, Michael Stein, David Silva, Pitch Black, Dominick Salemi and Joe Payne for giving me permission to reprint the material.

I owe a huge debt of gratitude to Mark McLaughlin, Cristopher DeRose, Amy Grech and Terrie Leigh Relf, my collaborators on some of these interviews.

Many thanks to editorial Wonder Woman Joan Mauch. She do the monster task of editing the book, helped me organize the manuscript and offered some great critiques on how to improve the quality of the book.

And I couldn't have done this book with the technical support from my friend and collaborator Mark McLaughlin, who spent many grueling hours transferring color photos to jpg and tif files. The finished photos really shine. Besides co-writing many articles, Mark helped edit the book and gave it the much needed finesse. Great job, buddy.

Thanks to Alan Dean Foster for writing the preface and Gregory Lamberson for writing the afterword.

Lastly, I'd like to thank my wife, Cindy, who traveled with me on this journey, helping with the difficult task of transcribing, proofreading, going to book signings and believing in me again.

Foreword
by Alan Dean Foster

Welcome to the circus.

Here there are no ringmasters: only acts. Within these pages you'll find a glistening, glittering, bombastic three-ring extravaganza. All ages are represented and all genders; masters and mistresses of the high-wire of film, the acrobatics of the written word, the mesmeric mysteries of television. Some acts are new, some venerable, some famous, some less so, but none are less than interesting to those with a mind that has not yet been dulled to the cognitive consistency of tepid tapioca by a numbing diet of pernicious politics, vapid "best-selling" fiction, screaming radio hosts (if they're the hosts, then who are the parasites?), howling televangelists convinced God must be deaf, sniggering Ponzi promoters with millions safely sequestered in off-shore banks, wars whose underlying rationales a coterie of inebriated chimps would find embarrassing, and a news media whose most famous and trusted name is a professional comedian.

And to think there are those with the gall to stand forth and decry as disengaged the aficionados of fantasy.

Beset by a lollygagging libido? Herein be regaled by the tales of those Tinseltown temptresses for whom tripping the light fantastic means avoiding gashing ones' feet to bloody ribbons on rows of shattered lightbulbs, to whom the theatrical admonition to break a leg is sometimes a command to the on-set makeup artist, and for whom the phrase "Director's cut" (which should please John Carpenter or Fred Olen Ray) takes on entirely new meaning.

The travails of daily life getting you down? Society says gulp a handful of pills. Better to heed the work and recommendations of the writers interviewed in this worthy tome. Their words will make you feel better, put pep in your step, stimulate the one organ of your body that raises you above the rats in your walls, and prove addictive without being narcotic.

Alan Dean Foster on the road out of Marrakech, heading into the Atlas Mountains of Morocco. The sign gives the directions from Marrakech to Ouarzazate (a major town in the Moroccan Sahara) (photograph by James Gurney, November 2008).

Yes, it's a grand old circus on offer here, whose antecedents stretch back to the time of Gilgamesh and back to the Neolithic cave painters, whose sequential portraits of running aurochs and woolly rhinos presage by thousands of years the work of the inimitable Ray Bradbury — see Ring Number Two where the acrobats are gathered.

But this circus is not free. There are requirements beyond the modest shekels you must shell out. To get in, you must perforce open your mind as much as your wallet. Entry requires a dollop of intelligence, a modicum of daydreaming, and a desire to explore that which lies beyond the humdrum (which itself lies in a nebulous zone somewhere between the timpani and the snares, and must forever be played pianissimo).

That's why this book is called *Masters of Imagination*. Come one, come all. I can't be the ticket-taker but I'm proud to stand forth, however briefly, as barker.

Alan Dean Foster is a popular and prolific writer of science fiction, fantasy, dark fantasy and horror. His media tie-in novelizations include those for Star Wars, Star Trek, *and the* Alien *trilogy.*

Preface

It seems like a badly clichéd episode of *The Twilight Zone*: The embattled author (of course played by a sweaty William Shatner) is forced to write his own obituary. That's what I'm doing right now, of a sort. I'm not dying, but this is the last book of interviews I'm writing.

"Mike, why would you not want to write any more books of interviews?" you might ask.

The answer is this: I feel you should always leave when you are at the top of your game. And with this collection of interviews with horror, science fiction and fantasy writers and filmmakers, I am on the top. Twenty-five interviews with the biggest names in the genre including Ray Bradbury, John Carpenter, Laurell K. Hamilton, Joe Lansdale, Ingrid Pitt, Linnea Quigley, Thomas Ligotti and more.

Masters of Imagination is my fifth book of interviews, after *Giants of the Genre* (Wildside Press, 2003), *More Giants of the Genre* (Wildside Press, 2005), *Modern Mythmakers* (McFarland, 2008) and *Esoteria-Land* (Bear Manor Media, 2009).

Masters of Imagination is the first book I've written just for my fans. Following book signings, lectures, guest appearances, etc., many of my readers have requested I do some of the interviews included in this collection. I hope you are satisfied with the result. Another fan request was to include behind-the-scenes stories about the interviews, and here are a few of them.

Ray Bradbury

Ray is a master storyteller and the short story is where he reigns. For over half a century, no author has been more respected for or prolific with the short story.

I remember the first story I read by him. I was in tenth grade and Mr. Cervantes, the English teacher, assigned us to read "The Smile," a dark tale about a future society where a boy waits in line to spit on a painting of the Mona Lisa.

My life was forever changed. Years later, I found out that Ray Bradbury was coming to the Quad Cities. So I prepared some questions just in case he would grant me an interview. After he gave a lecture at Augustana College, I approached Mr. Bradbury and asked if I could interview him. He said no, because that was the closest he'd ever been to the Mississippi River and he wanted to go take a look. However, he did give me his number and said I could do an interview over the phone.

That was my first interview with Ray. I interviewed him again for *Modern Mythmakers*. I feel like the luckiest man on Earth to have interviewed Ray Bradbury twice.

Linnea Quigley

Linnea was born in my hometown of Davenport, Iowa. She used to watch *Acri Creature Feature* just like I did when I was growing up. She left the Quad Cities, moved to Hollywood and became a scream queen icon. You gotta love a lady for that.

I remember the first film I saw that Linnea was in. I was going to college at the University of Iowa. I talked my friend Scott Madsen into cutting some classes and going to see a horror movie called *The Return of the Living Dead*.

Linnea played this red-headed punk named Trash. In a graveyard she delivered the infamous speech: "Do you ever wonder about all the different ways of dying? And wonder, like, what would be the most horrible way to die? For me, the worst way of dying would be for a bunch of old men to get around me, and start biting and eating me alive. First they would tear off my clothes...." She then started stripping.

I actually spilled my bucket of hot-buttered popcorn. Over the years I would enjoy watching her in such films as *Night of the Demons, Hollywood Chainsaw Hookers* and *Innocent Blood* without spilling any more of my popcorn.

I remember seeing an early film of hers, *Silent Night, Deadly Night* (I have a warm spot in my heart, or elsewhere, for her "Best Impaled-on-Antlers" performance in that film). I met Linnea while she was filming the movie *Unaware* in Galena, Illinois, and hit her up with a short story idea called "The Wizard of Ooze." She gave me a lot of innovative input and later we bounced more thoughts back and forth over the phone and the Internet. The resulting story ended up in the Cemetery Dance anthology that featured short fiction by horror actors and actresses. You can read it in *Midnight Premiere* or my own short story collection, *Little Creatures*.

We are talking about writing a novel together next....

Charles L. Grant

The first time I met Charles L. Grant was at the World Horror Convention in Denver when he received his Bram Stoker Award for Lifetime Achievement.

It was a hectic time for me. I was trying to pin Neil Gaiman down for an interview with *Science Fiction Weekly* (which did happen about a year later) and convince Harlan Ellison to do an interview with me for *Gallery* (which didn't happen at all).

In between all of that, I talked with Charles about possibly doing an interview sometime down the road for *Hellnotes*. He was very polite and said that he'd like to do an interview. I took his telephone number, put it into one of my notebooks and forgot about it. Then about three years later, I was talking on the phone to my friend and collaborator, Cristopher DeRose, about possible interviewees and he mentioned that one of his favorite writers in speculative fiction was Charles L. Grant.

At that point, I said something like, "Oh, no! I was supposed to do an interview with him three years ago." So I called up Charles to do an interview. He was still polite, even through I was over 1,095 days late.

Christopher Moore

The first person I thought about interviewing for *Masters of Imagination* was Christopher Moore. I am such a huge fan of his work. My interview with Christopher in *Modern Mythmakers* was good, but I thought we could do an even better one, and I think we have.

Also, when I did the interview this time, he wasn't on the road doing signings and lectures for his book *You Suck*. This time around, Christopher agreed to do an exclusive interview for this book, which was very kind. (I also have to thank Nancy Holder and William F. Nolan for doing the same thing.)

Laurell K. Hamilton

I'm a big fan of Laurell K. Hamilton's vampire books. I love bloodsucker books in general, but the Anita Blake vampire series is unique — highly imaginative, sexy and scary. She throws everything into her best-sellers — mystery, fantasy, magic, horror and romance. Anita's personal and professional relationships with a master vampire and an alpha werewolf heat up this serial.

I met Laurell at the World Horror Convention in Kansas City where she was the toastmistress of ceremonies. I really enjoyed her panel about vampires with another genre giant, Chelsea Quinn Yarbro (creator of the famous St. Germain series) and John Wooley (author of a great vampire book called *Awash in the Blood*).

She had long dark hair and wore dark sunglasses and a black and red flowered dress. She looked just as mysterious and magnetic as her Anita Blake character. Laurell was also considerate enough to give in to such requests as posing for a photo with me at the convention.

I've done a couple of interviews with this best-selling author and I immensely enjoy talking with her. Laurell K. Hamilton holds nothing back during the Q&As. She gives it all to her legion of fans — you have to love that quality in an interviewee.

John Carpenter

I remember the first film I saw by John Carpenter was *Halloween*. At that time, I was underage and couldn't get into an R-rated movie. I kept seeing the spooky commercials for the fright feature and wanted badly to see it. Then I read in the newspaper that on Halloween night a local theater was giving a dollar discount if you wore a costume to the show. I wore my dad's coveralls, some boots and a Frankenstein mask. I was able to sneak in and save a buck, too.

I sat in the dark theater and from the point where a six-year-old Michael Myers, wearing a clown mask, stalks his sister, until the creepy conclusion, I had the bejesus scared out of me. Twenty-five years later it still scares the bejesus out of me.

I'm a huge fan of John Carpenter; he is one of the most talented and ingenious filmmakers in the horror and science fiction genres. A screenwriter as well as a director, he is responsible for classics such as *The Fog, Escape from New York, Starman, Christine* (that book was a big influence on my own novel *Monster Behind the Wheel*), *They Live, Memoirs of an Invisible Man, Body Bags, John Carpenter's Vampires* and *Ghosts of Mars*.

I feel *Masters of Imagination* is a follow-up of sorts to *Modern Mythmakers*. Both books feature interviews with some of the same names: Ray Bradbury, Peter Straub, William F. Nolan, Joe Lansdale, Laurell K. Hamilton and Christopher Moore. The reason I interviewed these people again is that their careers are too big to cover with just one interview. If you like *Masters of Imagination*, by all means, seek out *Modern Mythmakers*. I am sure you will enjoy that book as well. I really enjoyed writing both and hope you will enjoy reading them.

It is great to have a genre giant like Alan Dean Foster write the foreword to this book. Alan is one of the rare people I have interviewed in all my books, so his involvement is an honor. Likewise with Gregory Lamberson, whom I met at two Bram Stoker award ceremonies (June 2009, Burbank, California).

Masters of Imagination is for my fans, old as well as new. I hope you enjoy it because it is the book of interviews that I have always wanted to do. It has everything I always wanted to put into a book: twenty-five interviews, author's notes, great photos (some rare), filmographies, bibliographies, award listings and an index. What do I hope the fans get from this book? The feeling that they have sat down with all twenty-five of these interviewees and shared their insights into books and movies.

Unlike at a funeral where a eulogy would typically be read, this is not really a sad occasion, but a happy one. I feel I've done a great job with both *Masters of Imagination* and *Modern Mythmakers*. Now I am exiting gracefully. It's like my analogy to *The Twilight Zone* at the beginning of this preface: I'm moving into a new dimension, but I'll still be read in reruns.

"My favorite ending is from Hugo's *The Hunchback of Notre Dame*. If you've only seen the Hollywood film versions where they let Esmeralda live, you don't know the power of the original. Esmeralda dies. Then Quasimodo finds her in the tomb, curls up with her corpse in his arms, and stays there until he also dies. We know this because years later two skeletons, one hunchbacked and misshapen, are found entwined, and when they try to separate his from hers, it crumbles to dust."

— *C. Dean Anderson*

I Am Dracula: C. Dean Andersson

C. Dean Andersson is the internationally published author of the 2007 Bram Stoker Finalist short story "The Death Wagon Rolls On By." His horror novels include groundbreaking vampire classics I Am Dracula *and* Raw Pain Max *and the controversial* Torture Tomb *pitting Feminist Witches against snuff filmmakers. In* Heroic Fantasy, *he created the Bloodsong Saga (*Warrior Witch, Warrior Rebel, *and* Warrior Beast*), a Sword and Sorcery epic published in American editions and Russian-language hardbacks. Trained from childhood in music, and with diverse degrees in physics, astronomy and art, he is also a professional artist, musician, robotics programmer and mainframe computer technical writer. His website is: www.cdeanandersson.com.*

What can you tell us about the short story "Mama Strangelove's Remedies for Afterlife Disorders or How I Learned to Stop Worrying and Love Mother Death"?

It occurred to me that if you died in one of the real-life horrors raging today in Iraq, and if you did so without strong ties to any particular deity, it would make mythological sense to find the dreaded Sumerian Death Goddess, Ereshkigal, waiting on the Other Side, because Iraq in ancient times was Sumeria. And since the war in Iraq reminds me of the Vietnam conflict, it seemed right to use a '60s-style title, based upon an obvious Kubrick movie source. Then, combined with the drawing of the Horned Goddess, it all came together in a short story. One of the Sumerian words associated with Goddesses, by the way, is "Mama," meaning "Mother."

My Muses tend to be the deities that most of today's prevalent mythologies either condemn and denigrate or ignore and try to forget. The strong and dangerous, so-called Dark Goddesses have, therefore, inspired much of my work. Fans of the status quo that sees males as superior to females find such Goddesses especially threatening, and the kinds of horror and dark fantasy I prefer challenge that status quo. The Norse Death Goddess, Hel, Loki's daughter, has been in my Bloodsong books and other stories several times, along with Freyja, Shamaness — Goddess of War, Magic, and Love. Coming from farther south, the Greek Triple Goddess — Hecate, that Crossroads Goddess beloved by Witches and dramatized by Shakespeare, consented to appear with Her Priestess, Medea, in *Fiend*. The rebel Sumerian Goddess, Tiamat, came to the rescue in *I Am Dracula*. The Babylonian Demoness, Lamashtu, regained her Goddesshood from atop the Matterhorn in *The Lair of Ancient Dream*. And returning to the northlands, the Giantess-Goddess Skadi aided Frankenstein's Creation, a reincarnated Viking, in *I Am Frankenstein*.

I do not recall encountering a mythological reference to Ereshkigal's possessing horns and snakes for hair, by the way, but mythologically horns and snakes are associated with ancient power and wisdom, the Earth, and the Underworld, so they fit. And since I'm still breathing, Queen Ereshkigal was evidently not horribly offended.

Why do you write horror?

I find it fun, for starters, and these days. I don't want to waste time on fiction writing that is not fun. Thinking back, while in elementary school, I once gave a speech, complete with crayon drawings as illustrations, to my grandmother's church group. I'd read a book on UFOs and seen *The Thing* on TV, so I was trying to scare them into realizing the danger of space aliens. I warned them, "Keep watching the skies!" Their reaction was to think me awfully cute. But the trait that motivated me then is still with me: to show people things they've never seen, give them thoughts they've never had and feelings they've never experienced, all while having some fun telling a good story. If I need an artsy excuse for my motivation, I can quote Tristan Tzara's 1918 *Dada Manifesto*: "Art should be a monster that casts servile minds into terror."

Of course, I should also warn you that waking up people can make them grumpy, especially if new ideas do not validate their previously cherished beliefs, so if you're not merely thought to be cute, you might become unpopular. On the other hand, those people are probably not reading stories like mine anyway. That's show biz!

I Am Dracula: C. Dean Andersson • 11

Vampire and fantasy writer C. Dean Andersson at the Temple of Sekhmet at Cactus Springs, Nevada, near Las Vegas (photograph by Nina Romberg, 2008).

Do you have a sense if a book is going to be successful or not? What books surprised you by their success?

If you're happy with what you create, that's success. But as for what becomes of a story when it's released into the world and the publishing industry takes over, does any writer have a clue? My version of the Countess Bathory story *Raw Pain Max* had good sales potential in the days when horror novels were booming and boundaries in horror fiction were being demolished. Splatterpunk was on the horizon. Then, surprise! A major book chain passed on carrying *Raw Pain Max* not because of the content, but because the excellent J.K. Potter cover art did not appeal to the chain's book buyer, which cut the publisher's bottom-line enthusiasm, advertising budget, and the print run. Afterward, I wondered if anyone had found and read *Raw Pain Max* at all. Those were pre–Internet days. Couldn't Google it. Then a woman at a convention thanked me for writing *Raw Pain Max* and said that reading it had helped her, because reading it had been like reading her own autobiography. At another convention, a woman who'd worked as a stripper wanted me to help with her memoir, because *Raw* made her think I could understand the hell she'd been through. And at a World Fantasy Con, I met an excellent artist who told me he'd had his girlfriend read to him from *Raw Pain Max* to inspire him while he painted. Another *Raw Pain Max* surprise came when I attended my first World Horror Convention. Without my being aware of it, *Raw* had become what one dealer called a "cult classic." He had a big price on the used paperback copy he was selling. And other writers I respected told me they were fans of the book. Now it's been requested that I have the book reprinted. Good idea. So, I checked with *Raw*, and when I find the right publisher, she'll be happy to dust off her whips and chains, kick-start her Harley, and ride again.

The Lair of Ancient Dreams is a historical Lovecraftian horror fantasy novel. Do you still enjoy and find inspiration in H.P. Lovecraft's work? And if Lovecraft were alive today, what would he be doing for a living?

Yes, his work still inspires. As for what Lovecraft would be doing for a living today, after he'd written a daily blog on astronomy and another on literature, he might go to a day job as a tech writer. Technical documentation has a lot in common with imaginative fiction. You have to make difficult concepts and improbable things believable and understandable. Speaking of H.P. Lovecraft, if you ever hoped or feared that Cthulhu and company were more than just fiction, give Kenneth Grant's books a try, such as *Outside the Circles of Time*, *Hecate's Fountain*, *Cults of the Shadow*, *Nightside of Eden* and *Outer Gateways*. He treats the Old Ones as an occult reality. They're difficult books to read if you're like me and not a specialist trained in the terminology, methodology, and poetry of Crowley-esque, Left-Hand Path Qabalistical Magick. But Grant is worth the effort. Good food for deep thoughts, deep and dark.

You've written about vampires in your books *I Am Dracula*, *Crimson Kisses*, and *Raw Pain Max*. Are vampire books easier or harder to write than other genre books?

We're not talking about selling a vampire novel to a publisher here. You'd have to ask an agent or editor about that. But writing a novel is never easy, no matter the genre. It can be fun, and it had better be, or chances are it will never get finished, in my case at least, but it's always hard work, seems to me, if you're doing it right, going back and doing adequate self-editing, all of that. But with the hordes of vampire books in print now, if you develop a unique outlook, anything you write should also be unique. And if vampire stories are something you're into, something that's fun for you to write about and explore, then go forth and stick to it and do it. No publisher's stake has yet been able to make the vampire genre die. It's an ancient human fear and fascination that keeps coming back in new ways. Find one of those new ways, and it should not be any harder to write a vampire novel than any other kind. Your own book, *Liquid Diet*, is a good example of finding a different and entertaining approach.

Thank you for the kind words about *Liquid Diet: Vampire Satire* and thanks for writing the afterword to that book as well. What are some of your favorite vampire books?

My favorite will always be Bram Stoker's original *Dracula*. I've read it several times. Always brings back the creepy feeling I got the first time I read it as a kid. After *Dracula*, my next two favorites are Richard Matheson's *I Am Legend* and Theodore Sturgeon's *Some of Your Blood*. Add Stephen King's loving homage to the genre, *Salem's Lot*, of course. I also enjoyed the novelization of *Dracula's Daughter*, written by Ramsey Campbell, I believe, under the pen name of Carl Dreadstone. [The movie] *Dracula's Daughter* was my first childhood encounter with vampires. I saw it one night late on TV. Still love watching it. Gloria Holden was perfect. And that great last line intoned by Edward Van Sloan's Van Helsing, "She was beautiful when she died ... a hundred years ago."

Why did you choose to write about Dracula and Erzebet Bathory?

I've already mentioned that Stoker's *Dracula* remains my favorite vampire novel, but nothing ever satisfied me, in fiction or nonfiction studies of vampire beliefs, regarding exactly how Dracula became a vampire. So, I ended up writing my own explanation. And I became fascinated by Countess Bathory in childhood after reading about her in William Seabrook's *Witchcraft*. As a writer, I wondered how a modern woman might deal with discovering she was the reincarnation of Erzebet, a Hungarian noblewoman who killed and tortured hundreds of young women, and how that former life might be influencing her current life as a whip-wielding, live-sex S&M stage performer called Raw Pain Max who is driven by the same urges that drove Erzebet. Does she fight those dark and violent needs? Give in to them like Erzebet did? Or find a way to transform them into fantasies? That's the struggle.

I Am Dracula **is an epic** vampire novel about Vlad the Impaler and his struggle with Satan, stretching over five centuries. Did this novel involve a lot of research into Vlad?

Yes. I studied *In Search of Dracula* and the other books about Prince Vlad written by the historians McNally and Florescu, and also Leonard Wolf's notes in his *Annotated Dracula*. I also re-read Stoker's *Dracula* and many nonfiction books about vampires, too — the Montague Summers' classics, for example. *Crimson Kisses*, published in 1981, became one of the earliest "how-Vlad-became-a-vampire" novels, a hidden history of Vlad, showing how he became Stoker's Vampire King. This did not violate the known history of Stoker. Trouble was, *Crimson Kisses* had a cliffhanger ending that was meant to lead into a series of novels. But *Crimson Kisses* editor left the publisher, and the series did not happen. So, twelve years later I wrote *I Am Dracula*. The *Crimson Kisses* editor had preferred a third-person approach, so my original proposal, called *I Am Dracula* and written in first-person, had to be rewritten into third-person and retitled *Crimson Kisses*, with the invaluable help of an excellent, already published writer, Nina Romberg, under an androgynous pen name, "Asa Drake."

With *I Am Dracula*, I gave the story back its original title and rewrote it again, returned it to first-person, expanded *Crimson Kisses* ideas, revised it with updated knowledge, and resolved *Crimson Kisses*' cliffhanger ending.

One of my favorite characters in your books is Tzigane, who appears in both *I Am Dracula* and *Crimson Kisses*. What was the inspiration for this character? And will she ever appear in any short stories or novels in the future?

Victor Hugo's *The Hunchback of Notre Dame* is, after *Dracula*, the book I've re-read the most. The first film version I saw as a kid was the one starring Gina Lollobrigida as the Gypsy, Esmeralda. Looking back, that's probably Tzigane's origin. So, when I discovered that a tribe of Gypsies were Dracula's allies in Stoker's novel, I wondered why and speculated that maybe one of their own had initiated Vlad into vampirism, a proud and powerful Gypsy woman devoted to a cause she saw as vital and just. Tzigane also has a small but important role near the end of *I Am Frankenstein* and is mentioned in *Fiend* by the immortal Greek witch Medea, who knows her. Then, too, she's in the new Dracula novel I'm working on now. And remember, in *I Am Dracula* Vlad reveals that Stoker's *Dracula* was Tzigane's idea, and that she secretly and mischievously used hypnosis and telepathy to inspire and control Stoker's writing. So, it all comes full circle, and anything in Stoker that does not agree with the "truth" in *I Am Dracula* is therefore Tzigane's fault. That probably goes for accepted "history" too, and maybe movie versions. That hairdo Gary Oldman wore at the first of Coppola's *Bram Stoker's Dracula* looks to me like something Tzigane would have dreamed up, and then laughed her head off at the premiere. Vampire humor is tricky.

You have written *I Am Dracula* and *I Am Frankenstein*. Do you have any other classic monsters you would like to write in the *I Am...* format?

I was set to write *I Am the Mummy* and *I Am the Wolfman* next, but the publisher changed my editor, and the new one wanted everything I wrote to be traditional. Nothing wrong with that approach, but the term "creative differences" applied. So, things just didn't work out between us, and those books were not written. But I still might write them, and others, eventually, Tzigane willing. Yes, that's it. It was all Tzigane's fault! I would have played ball with that editor, but Tzigane refused, and I did not want a centuries-old vampire mad at me. Would you?

The Bloodsong Saga [*Warrior Witch*, *Warrior Rebel* and *Warrior Beast*] is an epic series. In the first one, Bloodsong comes back from the dead to work for the Death Goddess, Hel, because Hel is holding her daughter, Guthrun, hostage. In the second one, Bloodsong fights to rescue her daughter from Hel's forces, who want to awaken the dark magic Hel buried in Guthrun's soul. In the third one, Hel uses the powers Bloodsong helped her regain in the first book to invade the Lands of Life. With all of the warriors, shapeshifters, witches, gods and goddesses, how did you keep track of all the characters and places? Was it fun to write about Norse barbarian women warriors?

The characters and places mostly took care of themselves. Sometimes I looked back at a previous book to check on something, of course, but all three were written within a year and a half, so it all stayed fresh in my mind. Writing the books was fun because of my long-time interest in Norse mythology.

My father was born in Sweden, and so early on I became interested in Scandinavian themes. I began wearing a replica of a Viking Age Thor's Hammer medallion while I was in the Air Force. Years later, I discovered that others had begun doing that too, first in conjunction with the rebirth of the Old Norse religion called Asatrú, and later by Scandinavian rock musicians like the Swedish group Bathory, whose leader, the late Quorthon, invented the Viking Metal genre and dedicated a song to me because of my *Bloodsong Saga*, "One Rode to Asa Bay," on Bathory's *Hammerheart*. I'm proud of that. It's a fine song. But back to Bloodsong.

Norse myths had not been used as much in fantasy as the Celtic myths at the time Bloodsong was created, nor were women warriors often featured as lead characters in those days before *Xena* conquered TV and warrior women in heroic fantasies became the norm. You could still hear serious discussions by respected elder writers at conventions about whether a female character could ever be truly believable as a warrior. Bloodsong fought to save her daughter for the first time less than a year before Sigourney Weaver blew 'em away to save Newt in *Aliens* and then later a tough Linda Hamilton battled a Terminator to save her son in *Terminator 2*. The times they were a-changin' for the acceptance of strong women fighting back, and I'm proud Bloodsong was part of it.

What are your thoughts on the covers by artist Boris Vallejo?

They are all gorgeous and I thank him for doing such outstanding work for Bloodsong. Some people thought he exposed too much flesh on the women, but remember, he was boldly using female bodybuilders as models for my warrior women at a time when it was controversial to show women with muscles. Yes, there was such a time! And using bodybuilders for models wouldn't have made much sense if they'd been dressed in overcoats. Plus, Conan was always running around next to naked, muscles gleaming. On the other hand, I show on my website what the Russian artist, Ilia Voronin, did with Bloodsong on the covers of the Russian-language editions fifteen years later. His Bloodsong is a pumped-up, scarred, tattooed, and armor-clad warrior, just as magnificent as Boris' visions, but in a different way.

As you've mentioned, your *Bloodsong* books have been translated into different languages. Do you need to keep that international audience in mind as you write? Do you work closely with any of the translators?

No. The Russian publisher, Alpha-Kniga, translated the Bloodsong books without any involvement from me. Someone who knows Russian read some passages to me, though, and it was close to the English. Maybe the Russian audiences liked them because of the old Scandinavian connection. Some Vikings, in particular Swedes, went east into Russia. There are historians who think the name Russia came from a name given to those Swedish Vikings, "rus," meaning "red," referring to their reddish-blond hair. They were traders, mainly, and established trading towns such as Kiev and Novgorod.

Happy endings in novels: good, bad, and indifferent?

Anything goes, as long as it works. I usually prefer there to be at least some hope of a happy ending. But one of my favorite endings is from Hugo's *The Hunchback of Notre Dame*. If you've only seen the Hollywood film versions where they let Esmeralda live, you don't know the power of the original. Esmeralda dies. Then Quasimodo finds her in the tomb, curls up with her corpse in his arms, and stays there until he also dies. We know this because years later two skeletons, one hunchbacked and misshapen, are found entwined, and when they try to separate his from hers, it crumbles to dust. That ending still gets me. But there are also those wonderful endings like in Arthur C. Clarke's *Rendezvous with Rama* and his *Childhood's End* and his "Nine Billion Names of God" and his "The Star." And at the end of Richard Matheson's *The Shrinking Man*, endings that leave you clutched by a deep sense of wonder and/or gasping with surprise. I love those, too. And the last page of Graham Masterton's *Tengu* is an ending I admire simply because it's totally merciless, in a mega-doom kind of way. There are also endings that are only happy ones from a certain viewpoint. Was the ending to Stoker's *Dracula* a happy one if you were hoping Count Dracula would escape Van Helsing's gang? Considering Tzigane was behind it, though, we could look upon it as just another of her happy little vampire jokes.

Last words?

Thanks for giving me the chance to urge everyone one more time to please, please, "Keep watching the skies!" Because those long-dead, ex-church-going ex-grandmothers from my small hometown still think I'm awfully cute, according to Tzigane. What more could a horror writer ask?

Books by C. Dean Andersson

NOVELS

Crimson Kisses (1981) (writing as Asa Drake) (with Nina Romberg)
Lair of Ancient Dreams (1982) (writing as Asa Drake) (with Nina Romberg)
Torture Tomb (1987)
Raw Pain Max (1988)
Buried Screams (1992)
I Am Dracula (1993) (A second edition of *I Am Dracula* was published in 1998.)
Fiend (1994)
I Am Frankenstein (1996)

BLOODSONG SAGA

Warrior Witch (2000)
Warrior Rebel (2000)
Warrior Beast (2000)

HEL (writing as Asa Drake)

Warrior Witch of Hel (1985)
Death Riders of Hel (1985)
Werebeasts of Hel (1986)

The *Hel Trilogy* was republished in 2000 by Hawk Books in trade paperback format under the name C. Dean Andersson. The 2000 versions had introductions that he wrote especially for each and were retitled as *Warrior Witch, Warrior Rebel, Warrior Beast.*

The three books were published again by a Russian publisher, Alpha Kniga, in 2002 as Russian language hardbacks with new cover paintings, front-piece art, and end paper art by Russian artists.

"I love Billie in *Creepshow*. She's one of my all-time favorite characters. And I really didn't know what I was doing when I showed up for work. I just told George [Romero] I was going to do what I thought would work for her and if he didn't like it, he'd better send me home immediately. It was a new experience for me because she was so over-the-top."

— *Adrienne Barbeau*

"A Real Gun-Totin', Ghost-Fightin' Heroine": Adrienne Barbeau

by Mark McLaughlin and Michael McCarty

Actress Adrienne Barbeau first came to the attention of national audiences in the role of the outspoken daughter Carol in the hit TV series Maude. *More recently, TV audiences have seen her portray Oswald's mom on* The Drew Carey Show. *She is currently starring as Ruthie the snake dancer on the HBO series* Carnivàle. *Horror-suspense fans know her best from her performances in such films as* The Fog, Escape from New York, Swamp Thing, Creepshow, Burial of the Rats *(with Linnea Quigley),* Two Evil Eyes, *and* The Convent.

She has also been in a large number of made-for-television movies and made guests appearances on numerous shows including Love Boat, Fantasy Island, Terror at London Bridge *(written by William F. Nolan) and* Star Trek: Deep Space Nine. *In the 1990s she provided the voice of Cat Woman on* Batman: The Animated Series.

She made a country album called Adrienne Barbeau *in 1997 and is the author of two books. Her latest publication is* Vampyres of Hollywood *(co-written by Michael Scott), the first of a series of vampire novels for St. Martin's*

Press. Director George Romero called Vampyres of Hollywood *"[s]mart, witty, fast-paced, thoroughly entertaining."*

Where are you from? Are you considered a celebrity in your hometown?

I'm from all over California, primarily the Central Valley (the Armenian contingent in Fresno) and the Bay area (San Jose). I started working professionally with the San Jose Light Opera when I was 16 and so I am sort of known there as "hometown girl makes good." You can check my website, www.abarbeau.com, for more bio info.

You didn't start your career in suspense-horror. You were one of the stars of the popular sitcom *Maude*, which is pretty far from the horror field. *The Fog* was your first feature film and scary movie. What aspect of making horror films appeals to you?

Adrienne Barbeau, actress and author (photograph by Pamela Springfield, 2007).

Actually I didn't start my career with *Maude*. I started on Broadway in *Fiddler on the Roof* as Tevye's daughter, Hodel. And then went on to create the role of Rizzo in the original Broadway production of *Grease*.

What *doesn't* appeal to me about horror films is watching them. I'd much rather do them than see them. They're great fun to do because they provide an opportunity to express emotions we're not always dealing with in romances or comedies. I think what appeals to me most about the ones I've done has been the opportunity to work with the directors I've worked with. And to play a heroine, a real gun-totin,' ghost-fightin' heroine.

Your role as the gleefully shrewish wife in *Creepshow* was one of the movie's highlights. Do you have any anecdotes about that segment?

I love Billie in *Creepshow*. She's one of my all-time favorite characters. And I really didn't know what I was doing when I showed up for work. I just told George [Romero] I was going to do what I thought would work for her and if he didn't like it, he'd better send me home immediately. It was a new experience for me because she was so over-the-top. I just trusted George to know what would work and tried to give it to him. Actually, when I first read the script, I didn't get it at all. I thought it was horrendously gory and didn't think I wanted to be involved. Tommy Atkins had to explain to me that it was going to be shot like a comic book and I shouldn't take the script descriptions quite so literally.

You bring a lot of intensity to your roles, whether you're the DJ-concerned mother in *The Fog* or the gutsy town recluse in *The Convent*. Is this the product of your training as an actress, or do you feel a rapport with these characters?

I think I find a rapport with the characters I'm playing, I search for an understanding of them that resonates with me. Why they do the things they do — whether it's bitch at a miserable husband or help a teenager blow away nuns.

***The Convent* is a highly unconventional** horror movie, with lots of dark humor and an almost rock-video feel. What was your initial reaction when you were first presented with this script?

As soon as I got to the part of the *Convent* script where adult Christine makes her entrance, I knew I had to do it. I think it's a great hoot of a movie and was really sorry it didn't get a theatrical release in the States. Mike Mendez did a great job with a funny script and no money.

Which of your movies are you most proud of?

I guess I'm proudest of *Creepshow*, just because she's such an outlandish character and so far away from me and I managed to pull it off. I don't even drink. Never have. Don't like the taste of alcohol.

How much of your own stunt work do you do? Did you do any stunt work in *The Convent* or any of your other movies?

I do my own stunts whenever I can. I did the motorcycle driving in *The Convent*, swimming in the swamp in *Swamp Thing*, etc.

Were you creeped-out by the rats in *Burial of the Rats*? What frightens Adrienne Barbeau in real life?

The rats didn't bother me, although they weren't trained and they did bite. And I love working with the snakes in *Carnivàle*. The only thing that creeps me out is roaches. I wouldn't have done E.G. Marshall's scene in *Creepshow*, not for any amount of money. Or let's put it this way, I wouldn't have been acting.

It sounds like there's no shortage of excitement in your career. What has been your most unusual role so far?

What I'm most excited about these days is the second season of *Carnivàle*. That may not be my most unusual role but [it is certainly] unique. A snake dancer who has a romance with a young boy half her age, a boy who has the ability to heal and who brings her back from the dead. Can't beat that. I'm also excited about the two books I'm writing — a novel for all my horror fans and another, entitled *There Are Worse Things I Could Do*, that's a collection of stories from my life. The rats are prominently mentioned.

Movies & TV Moves with Adrienne Barbeau

Maude (1972–1978) TV
The Great Houdini (1976) TV
Hallmark Hall of Fame: Have I Got a Christmas for You (1977) TV
Quincy M.E. (1977) TV
Red Alert (1977) TV
Eight Is Enough (1977) TV
Someone's Watching Me! (1978) TV
Crash (1978) TV
Fantasy Island (1978–1983) TV
The Love Boat (1978) TV
Return to Fantasy Island (1978) TV
The Darker Side of Terror (1979) TV
The Fog (1980)
Tourist (1980) TV
Valentine Magic on Love Island (1980) TV
Top of the Hill (1980) TV
Charlie and the Great Balloon Chase (1981) TV
The Cannonball Run (1981)
Escape from New York (1981)
Creepshow (1982)
Swamp Thing (1982)
The Thing (1982) (uncredited) ... Computer
Hotel (1984–1986) TV
The Next One (1984)
Terror at London Bridge (1985) TV
The Twilight Zone (1985) TV
Seduced (1985) TV
Murder, She Wrote (1985–1987) TV
Back to School (1986)
Open House (1987)
Ultraman: The Adventure Begins (1987) TV
Monsters (1989) TV
Head of the Class (1989) TV

Cannibal Women in the Avocado Jungle of Death (1989)
CBS Schoolbreak Special: The Fourth Man (1990) TV
Two Evil Eyes (1990)
The Easter Story (1990)
Doublecrossed (1991) TV
Blood River (1991) TV
Batman (1992–1995) TV
Queen Esther (1992)
The Burden of Proof (1992) TV
Dream On (1992) TV
Daddy Dearest (1993) TV
Demolition Man (1993) (uncredited) (voice of Main Frame Computer)
Father Hood (1993)
ABC Weekend Specials: The Parsley Garden (1993) TV
FBI: The Untold Stories (1993) TV
Babylon 5 (1994) TV
The George Carlin Show (1994)
Jailbreakers (1994) TV
One West Waikiki (1994) TV
Silk Degrees (1994)
Burial of the Rats (1995) (TV)
The Wayans Bros. (1996) TV
Flipper (1996) TV
Weird Science (1997) TV
The New Batman Adventures (1997–1998) TV
The Drew Carey Show (1998–2004) TVv
Diagnosis Murder (1998) TV
A Champion's Fight (1998)
A Wake in Providence (1999)
The Angry Beavers (1998) TV
Scooby-Doo on Zombie Island (1998)
Sliders (1998) TV
Star Trek: Deep Space Nine (1999) TV
Inter Arma Enim Silent Leges (1999) TV
The Love Boat: The Next Way (1999) TV
Descent 3 (1999)
Batman Beyond (2000) TV
The Convent (2000)
Across the Line (2000)
Spring Break Lawyer (2001) TV
Nash Bridges (2001) TV
No Place Like Home (2001)
Totally Spies (2002–2004) TV
Carnivàle (2003–2005) TV
Ring of Darkness (2004) TV
The Santa Trap (2002) TV
The Chronicle (2002) TV
Gotham Girls (2002) TV
Ghost Rock (2004)

Christmas Do-Over (2006) (TV)
Marvel: Ultimate Alliance (2006)
Deceit (2006) (TV)
K-Ville (2007) TV
Unholy (2007)
Cold Case (2008) TV
Wings (2008) TV
Fly Me to the Moon (2008)
Dexter (2009) TV
Living the Dream (2009) TV
Batman: Arkham Asylum (2009)
Alice Jacobs Is Dead (2009)
Reach for Me (2009)
War Wolves (2009) TV
The Dog Who Saved Christmas (2009) TV
Grey's Anatomy (2010) TV
Complacent (2010) TV
The New Adventures of Old Christine (2010) TV
General Hospital (2010) TV

Books by Adrienne Barbeau

There Are Worst Things I Could Do (nonfiction) (2006)
Vampyres of Hollywood (novel) co-written with Michael Scott (2008)

"First of all, I'm a library person. I never made it to college — so I went to the library two or three days a week during my late teens and twenties. I know libraries well. I heard they were in danger; when Hitler burned the books in Germany in the mid-thirties; when I heard rumors of what Russia was doing with the books and authors — they were burning books too. They kept it quiet — but the word got out."

— *Ray Bradbury*

The Library Man: Ray Bradbury

When you hear the name Ray Bradbury, several images come to mind: a barren Martian landscape, a magical carnival in the Midwest and firemen burning stacks of books in the near future.

Bradbury is a legend in speculative fiction — and with good reason. His books have withstood the test of time, and are just as popular now as when they were first written. Science fiction, fantasy and horror genre fans have all embraced his works.

He wrote such classics as The Martian Chronicles, The Illustrated Man, Something Wicked This Way Comes, The October Country *and* Fahrenheit 451 *which is probably one of the most powerful books about literacy in science fiction (the book tells of a future age when literacy has become illegal and books and the book-lovers are burned). His latest is* Dawn to Dusk: Cautionary Travels, *published by Gauntlet Press.*

To learn more about Bradbury, read this Barry Hoffman interview. Hoffman's Gauntlet Press has published several of Bradbury's books over the years.

A lot of your books have been turned into movies. Which are some of your favorites?

The best one so far is *Something Wicked This Way Comes*. It has flaws, but it's darn good. Of course, I'm very proud of *Moby Dick*, which I wrote for [director] John Huston. I'd spent almost a year adapting [Herman]

Melville's novel. Beyond that, *The Ray Bradbury Theatre* has been on the air now for the last eight or nine years. I wrote 65 scripts for that, and they've come out very well. Out of the 65, they had only three clinkers. That's a good track record.

In *Something Wicked This Way Comes*, Jason Robards bears an uncanny resemblance to you. Do you see a lot of yourself in the father character, Charles Halloway?

Oh, I think so, sure. If you read the book, all the characters are me. The two boys [Will Halloway and Jim Nightshade] are the two halves of myself—the light half and the dark half. The father is me in the library. The entire book is me.

Do you think *The Martian Chronicles* has been accepted by more fantasy fans than science fiction fans over the years?

Ray Bradbury, grandmaster of science fiction, and Tigger, one of his favorite cats, in the mid–1980s (photograph by Tom Victor).

It doesn't matter, they all read it. Cal Tech, M.I.T.—all the scientific colleges teach it and talk about it. It's pure fantasy, except one short story in it called "There Will Come Soft Rain." *The Martian Chronicles* is labeled science fiction but it's fantasy. People don't mind. The book is about the future—it's mythical. I took Greek mythology and Roman mythology and Egyptian mythology, brought them forward into our time and projected them into the future.

You're very vocal on the subject of censorship and book burnings. This is evident in your book *Fahrenheit 451.* Is there any event in your life that brought this about?

Well, sure. First of all, I'm a library person. I never made it to college—so I went to the library two or three days a week, during my late teens and twenties. I know libraries well. I heard they were in danger when Hitler burned the books in Germany in the mid-thirties; when I heard rumors of what

Russia was doing with the books and authors — they were burning books too. They kept it quiet — but the word got out. And the history of the Alexandria library, which had been burned at least three times, 2,000 or so years ago, twice by accident and once on purpose. When you hear things like this, this is terrible. Libraries are my home, my nest. Quite naturally I began writing about it.

What was the inspiration for *Dandelion Wine?*

I grew up in Northern Illinois — Waukegan, which is thirty-five miles north of Chicago. I lived there until I was fourteen. I remember all the wonder years quite well. My grandparents lived next door and one of my favorite uncles lived in yet a third house nearby. Between the two houses was my grandparent's house, which was filled with books: The *Oz* books, *Alice in Wonderland*, and fairy tales books. And my uncle's house had all the *Tarzan* books, all the *John Carter* [*on Mars*], *Warlord of Mars* books. Between the two, I had a wonderful library in one city block.

To what do you attribute the fact that your work has been successful in so many different genres?

It's pure genetics — it's the way I was born. I was curious about the theater, curious about writing poetry, curious about essays. I have always loved the mystery field. A lot of writers in my field don't care about theater and I grew up in the theater. They didn't care much about radio. I started my career acting on it when I was twelve years old. [Author's note: Bradbury sold his first script for radio, for *The George Burns and Gracie Allen Show*, at the age of fourteen.] I wrote for a lot of the radio shows in my twenties. It's natural for me, to do all these things. I have loved poetry all my life, so I've written twelve books of poetry. Other people in my field simply don't do those things.

Last question — what can you tell us about *From the Dust Returns?*

[*laughs*]: I've only been working on it for fifty years. This is the year I finally finished it. The book is a lot of short stories about this strange family who are like vampires.

I've written thirty other books in the meantime. I started this book way back in the forties. I started it when I was twenty-six years old, when I went to New York. I had a meeting with Charles Addams [creator of *The Addams Family*] — we'd planned on doing it as a film together. He got busy with his vampire family, and I got busy with mine and some other projects and never got around to finishing it.

Books by Ray Bradbury

NOVELS

The Martian Chronicles (1950)
The Illustrated Man (1951)
Fahrenheit 451 (1953)
Dandelion Wine (1957)
Something Wicked This Way Comes (1962)
The Halloween Tree (1972)
Death Is a Lonely Business (1985)
A Graveyard for Lunatics (1990)
Green Shadows, White Whale (1992)
From the Dust Returned (2001)
Let's All Kill Constance (2002)
Farewell Summer (2006)

COLLECTIONS

Dark Carnival (1947)
The Golden Apples of the Sun (1953)
The October Country (1955)
A Medicine for Melancholy (1959)
The Day It Rained Forever (1959)
The Small Assassin (1962)
R Is for Rocket (1962)
The Machineries of Joy (1964)
The Autumn People (1965)
The Vintage Bradbury (1965)
Tomorrow Midnight (1966)
S Is for Space (1966)
Twice 22 (1966)
I Sing the Body Electric (1969)
Ray Bradbury (1975)
Long After Midnight (1976)
"The Fog Horn" & Other Stories (1979)
One Timeless Spring (1980)
The Last Circus and the Electrocution (1980)
The Stories of Ray Bradbury (1980)
Dinosaur Tales (1983)
A Memory of Murder (1984)
The Wonderful Death of Dudley Stone (1985)
The Toynbee Convector (1988)
Classic Stories 1 (1990)
Classic Stories 2 (1990)
The Parrot Who Met Papa (1991)
Selected from Dark They Were, and Golden-Eyed (1991)
Quicker Than the Eye (1996)
Driving Blind (1997)

Ray Bradbury Collected Short Stories (2001)
The Playground (2001)
One More for the Road (2002)
Bradbury Stories: 100 of His Most Celebrated Tales (2003)
Is That You, Herb? (2003)
The Cat's Pajamas: Stories (2004)
A Sound of Thunder and Other Stories (2005)
The Dragon Who Ate His Tail (2007)
Now and Forever: Somewhere a Band is Playing & Leviathan '99 (2007)
Summer Morning, Summer Night (2007)
We'll Always Have Paris (2009)
Dawn to Dusk: Cautionary Travels (2010)

Partial List of Awards

O. Henry Memorial Award (1947–1948)
Aviation–Space Writers Association Award (1968)
Science Fiction Hall of Fame (1970)
World Fantasy Award (1977)
Balrog Award (1979)
The Gandalf Award (1980)
Prometheus Award (1984)
Nebula Award (1988)
Bram Stoker Award (1989) (2001)
Los Angeles Citizen of the Year Award (1995)
Medal for Distinguished Contribution to American Letters (2000)
National Medal of Arts Award (2004)

Bradbury also received the Benjamin Franklin Award in 1954, the Jules Verne Award in 1984, the Valentine Davies Award in 1984, an Emmy for the teleplay of *The Halloween Tree* and an Oscar nomination for his animated film *Icarus Montgolfier Wright*.

"The ultimate bogeyman? The ultimate unkillable thing? If one goes back and looks at Westworld, that picture involved a robot gunfighter that keeps coming back again and again. I copied a bit of that idea and added it to a horror film on Halloween night with teenagers. To make Michael Myers frightening, I had him walk like a man, not a monster."

— *John Carpenter*

Halloween and Beyond: John Carpenter
by Michael McCarty and Mark McLaughlin

John Carpenter has been thrilling and enthralling moviegoers for years with hits like Starman, John Carpenter's Vampires, John Carpenter's Ghosts of Mars *and many more. But certainly his greatest fame came from his 1978 film* Halloween, *which has spawned numerous sequels and countless imitators.*

Though most of Carpenter's heroes are men of action, he doesn't ignore the strength and valor of women. Laurie Strode, as portrayed by Jamie Lee Curtis in Halloween, *proved to be the only one brave enough and resourceful enough to subdue the relentless silent killer, Michael Myers.*

Carpenter was born in Carthage, New York, and raised in Bowling Green, Kentucky. He enjoyed westerns as a child, which may explain the stalwart outlook of most of his heroes, as well as the high-action energy he brings to his work. He attended Western Kentucky University and later enrolled in the University of Southern California's School of Cinema. As a student, he completed the 1970 short subject The Resurrection of Bronco Billy, *which won an Academy Award. He went on to direct* Dark Star, Assault on Precinct 13 *and then* Halloween, *which earned over $75 million worldwide on a budget of $300,000.*

Following Halloween, *he scored big with the suspense and horror hits* The

Fog, They Live, Prince of Darkness, Christine, Escape from New York, The Thing, Big Trouble in Little China, In the Mouth of Madness *and* Village of the Damned. *He has also ventured into other genres, including the comedy* Memoirs of an Invisible Man *and the sci-fi romance* Starman. *For TV, Carpenter directed the thriller* Someone's Watching Me, *the mini-series* Elvis *and the Showtime horror trilogy* John Carpenter Presents Body Bags. *As a screenwriter, Carpenter's credits include* Eyes of Laura Mars, Halloween II, The Philadelphia Experiment, Black Moon Rising, Meltdown *and the TV western,* El Diablo. *He co-authored the screenplay of* John Carpenter's Vampires *with Dan Jakoby and Dan Mazar from* Vampire$, *a novel by John Steakly.*

What did executive producer Irwin Yablans give you to start *The Babysitter Murders* [later known as *Halloween*] creatively and how did you and Debra Hill develop that into the script?

Irwin Yablans said, "I want a movie about babysitter murders, about a stalker, a killer going after babysitters." He thought that all teenagers could relate to that, because they all babysat at some point. So I said, "Okay fine." Debra and I outlined an idea and I went off and directed the TV movie *Somebody's Watching Me*. She wrote the first part of the script, and after I finished the TV movie, I came back and finished it. One day Yablans called me on the telephone and said, "Why not set the film on Halloween night and we'll call it *Halloween*. It had never been used as a title before.

Michael Myers — The Shape — is the ultimate bogeyman: unstoppable, without reason and yet based in humanity. How did you and Debra go about creating Michael?

The ultimate bogeyman? The ultimate unkillable thing? If one goes back and looks at *Westworld*, that picture involved a robot gunfighter that keeps coming back again and again. I copied a bit of that idea and added it to a horror film on Halloween night with teenagers. To make Michael Myers frightening, I had him walk like a man, not a monster.

Was Michael Myers' character history, as conveyed in the later films, part of your original Myers mythos.

Michael Myers' connection to [Laurie] was all made up in the later films because my business partners wanted to make sequels. I can't stop them from making sequels. For *Halloween II* I contributed a screenplay, but I didn't want to direct it.

Most of Michael Myers' victims were sexually active, while the one who eludes him, Laurie [Jamie Lee Curtis], is virginal. Were you trying to make some kind of statement about sex being deadly?

For over 30 years, people have brought up this so-called "sexual statement" issue. It has been suggested that I was making some kind of moral statement. Believe me, I'm not. In *Halloween*, I viewed the characters as simply normal teenagers. Laurie was shy and somewhat repressed. And Michael Myers, the killer, is definitely repressed. They have certain similarities.

Halloween sparked a glut of horror movies based on serial killers attacking on holidays, for example *Friday the 13th, My Bloody Valentine, Valentine's Day, Mother's Day*, etc. They say imitation is the sincerest form of flattery ... were you flattered?

I was flattered, but I took it not as much about me as money. One could make money and get a career going with a low-budget horror film about killers attacking on holidays. It is always flattering to have somebody copy you.

Director John Carpenter on location, c. 2000.

You shot some scenes for the TV broadcast of *Halloween* to help pad the running time, using the cast and crew from *Halloween II*. Why?

NBC purchased the right to show *Halloween* on network television. The minimum length requirement was 93 minutes, if I remember correctly. *Halloween* only lasted 88 or 89 minutes. So we had to pad it to get to the length NBC required. I just added a lot of foolish crap — nothing particularly good.

You produced and scored *Halloween 3: Season of the Witch*. That movie broke away from Michael's story. Was the intent at that point to release a stand-alone movie on October?

I wanted to get away from what I thought was the dead end of the original *Halloween* story. It's basically the same idea over and over again. Nothing

A cut above the rest. Jamie Lee Curtis trapped in the closet in *Halloween* (1978) (courtesy John Carpenter).

really changes. *Halloween 3* was an attempt for something new. I was wrong. The audience didn't want to see a change. They wanted the Shape. So the Shape is what they got.

What was your level of creative input with the other *Halloween* sequels?
After *3*, I didn't have any creative input. I just collected checks.

Aliens and monsters hidden among us—that's the theme behind your movies *Village of the Damned*, *The Thing* and *Ghosts of Mars*. The main sense of horror in these films seems to come from paranoia: No one can be trusted. Do you see that as a dominant source of fear in today's world?

Evil hiding among us is an ancient theme. Demonic possession has been with us for centuries. With the emergence of science fiction, this evil sometimes takes the form of malevolent aliens.

You've written, directed, scored the music, edited and produced several of your movies. How do you juggle so many responsibilities?

With great difficulty.

Escape from New York **and** ***Escape from L.A.*** are set in a distant police-state society. Do you feel the United States is headed that that direction?

I don't feel the U.S. will resemble the world that I portrayed in the *Escape* movies. Certain aspects of it, yes—but I doubt to the extent of the fictional country that Snake Plissken found himself in.

What are your thoughts on the horror and science fiction genres?

I've always had a fondness for horror and science fiction.

You worked extensively with the late Donald Pleasence. Do you have any stories about your years of working with him?

Donald Pleasence was a dear friend for many years. I admired him as an actor and loved working with him. He was one of the funniest men I've known.

Satan and the Anti-God, as depicted in *Prince of Darkness*, appear to be science fictional as well as supernatural. For example, the Anti-God is trapped in a mirror dimension, and the liquid life-form in the ancient canister acts like a contagious virus. Do you feel the supernatural might be, in fact, another form of science?

This is a difficult question. I personally don't believe in the supernatural. On the movie screen, the supernatural certainly can exist, but in real life, no. But most people on the planet have a deep hunger for supernatural meaning. One can't just ignore it. I combine science and the supernatural to tell a story, nothing more.

Ghosts of Mars also combines the supernatural and science fiction: ghosts of long-dead aliens possess modern Earthlings. Do you believe in life after death, as either a supernatural or scientific phenomenon?

I don't believe in life after death.

Is there a project you ever passed on that you now wish you hadn't?

No.

You played a coroner in *Body Bags*. Do you have any acting roles lined up in the future?

If anyone asks me, I'll do it.

What scares John Carpenter?

That is another question that I've been asked for the last 30 years. I have the same answer every time. What scares me is what scares you. We're all afraid of the same things. That's why horror is such a powerful genre. All you have to do is ask yourself what frightens you and you'll know what frightens me.

John Carpenter's Filmography

Director

Dark Star (1973)
Assault on Precinct 13 (1976)
Halloween (1978)
Someone's Watching Me! (1978) (TV)
Elvis (1979) (TV)
The Fog (1980)
Escape from New York (1981)
The Thing (1982)
Christine (1983)
Starman (1984)
Big Trouble in Little China (1986)
Prince of Darkness (1987)
They Live (1988)
Memoirs of an Invisible Man (1992)
Body Bags (1993) (TV) (segments "The Gas Station," "Hair")
Village of the Damned (1995)
In the Mouth of Madness (1995)
Escape from L.A. (1996)
Vampires (1998)
Ghosts of Mars (2001)
Masters of Horror (2005) "John Carpenter's Cigarette Burns"
Masters of Horror (2006) "Prolife"

Composer

The Resurrection of Broncho Billy (1970)
Dark Star (1973)
Assault on Precinct 13 (1976)

Halloween (1978)
The Fog (1980)
Halloween III: Season of the Witch (1983)
Christine (1983)
Big Trouble in Little China (1986)
Prince of Darkness (1987)
They Live (1988)
Body Bags (1993) (TV)
Village of the Damned (1995)
In the Mouth of Madness (1995)
Escape from L.A. (1996)
Vampires (1998)
Ghosts of Mars (2001)

WRITER

The Resurrection of Broncho Billy (1970)
Dark Star (1973)
Assault on Precinct 13 (1976)
Halloween (1978)
Eyes of Laura Mars (1978) (also story)
Someone's Watching Me! (1978) (TV)
The Fog (1980)
Escape from New York (1981)
Halloween II (1981)
Black Moon Rising (1986) (also story)
Prince of Darkness (1987) (as Martin Quatermass)
They Live (1988) (as Frank Armitage)
El Diablo (1990) (TV)
Blood River (1991)
Escape from L.A. (1996)
Vampires (1998)
Meltdown (1999) (story)
Silent Predators (1999)
Ghosts of Mars (2001)

ACTOR

The Fog (1980) (uncredited) ... Bennett (assistant at the church)
Escape from New York (1981) Policeman in Helicopter
The Thing (1982) (uncredited)... Norwegian video footage
Starman (1984) (uncredited) ... Man in Helicopter
Memoirs of an Invisible Man (1992) (as Rip Haight)... Helicopter Pilot
Body Bags (1993) (TV)... Coroner
Il Silenzio dei prosciutti (1994) ... Trench Coat Man ... aka *Silence of the Hams*
Village of the Damned (1995) (uncredited) ... Man at Phone Booth

Producer

Dark Star (1973)
Halloween II (1981)
Halloween III: Season of the Witch (1983)
The Philadelphia Experiment (1984) (executive)
Body Bags (1993) (TV) (executive)

Editor Filmography

The Resurrection of Broncho Billy (1970)
Assault on Precinct 13 (1976) (as John T. Chance)

Awards

Golden Scroll for Best Special Effects, *Dark Star* (1974)
Los Angeles Film Critics Association New Generation Award (1979)
Avoriaz Fantastic Film Festival Critics Award, *Halloween* (1979)
Avoriaz Fantastic Film Festival Critics Award, *The Fog* (1980)
Avoriaz Fantastic Film Festival Critics Award, *Princes of Darkness* (1987)
Cable Ace Award Writing a Movie or Miniseries *El Diablo* (1990)
George Pal Memorial Award (1996)
Saturn Award for Best Music, *Vampires* (1999)
Stiges — Cataloian International Film Festival Carnet Jove — Special Mention *Masters of Horror* for episode "John Carpenter's Cigarette Burns" (2006)
Bram Stoker Lifetime Achievement Award (2007)
Stiges — Cataloian International Film Festival Time-Machine Honorary Award (2008)

"[T]he copy editor ... said, 'Mulder wouldn't say that.' I wrote a note back and said, 'Look at the show, he's swearing all the time.' According to Chris Carter, I didn't get Mulder and Scully right. Carter said the two books (*Goblins* and *Whirlwind*) were 'noir,' which is dark, and he said *The X-Files* wasn't."
— *Charles L. Grant*

In a Dark Dream: Charles L. Grant
by Cristopher DeRose and Michael McCarty

Charles L. Grant has been writing classic quiet horror for 35 years. A three-time World Fantasy Award winner and International Horror Guild's Living Legend, he debuted with The Shadow of Alpha *in 1976 and went on to win SFWA's Nebula Award twice and receive the British Lifetime Achievement Award and a Bram Stoker's Lifetime Achievement Award from the Horror Writers Association.*

Charles can also be found under the pseudonyms of Kent Montana creator-humorist Lionel Fenn and Timothy Boggs, author of expansion novels regarding the Hercules *TV saga. He lived in New Jersey with his author-editor wife Kathryn Ptacek. He passed away on September 15, 2006.*

You were the recipient of the International Horror Guild's Living Legend Awards. What does that mean to you?

I think it means I must be ready to die [*laughs*]. I received three of them in two years. I don't know what to say. I'm pleased that they thought about me, whoever voted for these things. I'm not old enough for that kind of thing. I'm only 60. This is the kind of award you get when you are in your 70s and 80s. I'm not done yet. Because of what ails me, it takes me considerably longer to write than it used to.

For *Nightsong*, did you have to research the occult or did you just create mythology according to what the plot required?

[*laughs*]: Ed Bryant always says, "I never do research, I just make it up." Almost, but not quite true. I wanted to do a zombie novel based on real zombies, not the George Romero kind of zombies. I did some research to make sure that my idea of zombies wasn't all taken from the movies.

Charles L. Grant standing in front of his gazebo at home (photograph by Mary Jasch, 2002).

What came first for *Symphony*, the plotline or the personification of the apocalypse?

The idea came first. It was the only commercial idea I had in my whole life and it flopped. I wanted to do four books each based on the Four Horseman. I wanted each of the Four Horseman to be different than anyone has ever thought of them before. That is why you got a woman, a kid, a guy who looks remarkably like Willie Nelson and an old black woman. I didn't want flowing robes or literally riding horses — or at least not until the end. I pitched that idea to my editor who loved it and the publisher loved it. It took me about five years to write the series.

Is Ethan Protor from the Black Oak series based on a real person specifically debunking the supernatural?

The idea was I could do *The X-Files* better than *The X-Files*. Unlike *The X-Files*, I wouldn't be making it up as I went along. This was the idea of a British editor who asked my agent if I ever thought about doing an *X-Files*–type series. And I hadn't at the time. As soon as it was mentioned, I thought I could do that, I could have fun and do all kinds of different things.

I gave the British editor my proposal and that SOB turned it down. But my editor at ROC up picked it. I projected a 12- or 13-book series with one whole story that would take three or four novels to tell, just like a TV show. I based it on that story arc business. Plus one story that would begin and end in each book. I loved it, I had a great time. I had not gotten such mail on any of my books or my entire career — when ROC killed it halfway through.

I'm hoping to get it done somehow. The sixth book is halfway done, it wouldn't take much to get that finished. I don't outline, I never did. But I set things up for each book in the series. It will probably have to be a small press that is willing to take a chance on it, because the major publishers won't pick it up.

In the *X-File* book *Goblins*, the supporting characters and Scully's interaction with them ... was that your own creation or was that something specified by Chris Carter?

Everything in those books except Scully and Mulder are mine. Carter kept his hands off, except to fire me. He didn't like them.

TV shows don't generally use much profanity. Were you comfortable adding that element to *Goblins*? Were there any concerns from Carter or the Fox Network because of that?

Nobody said anything, except the copy editor who said, "Mulder wouldn't say that." I wrote a note back and said, "Look at the show, he's swearing all the time." According to Chris Carter, I didn't get Mulder and Scully right. Carter said the two books [*Goblins* and *Whirlwind*] were "noir," which is dark, and he said *The X-Files* wasn't.

What would you consider your favorite, most perfect book and why?

There is none. I'm not satisfied with anything that I have done. I don't read them when they come out because I'm not going to like them. The only thing I do is, after they are published, I check the beginning to see if they got the beginning right and to make sure they haven't screwed up the ending. By the time the book is out of our house, I don't ever want to see it again [*laughs*]. I'll just read a paragraph and say, "That's awful, why did I write it that way?"

Last words?

There you go again, I'm not dead yet [*laughs*]. I wish more people would buy my books, so I can keep on writing. It's kind of doubtful these days. My goal has always been the same since the day I started out. Which is, not to scare anyone but to make them really, really nervous. Lifetime achievement awards or not, they are going to have to kill me to stop me from writing [*laughs*].

Books by Charles L. Grant

The Ravens of the Moon (1978)
A Quiet Night of Fear (1981)
The Nesting (1982)

Night Songs (1984)
The Tea Party (1986)
For Fear of the Night (1988)
In a Dark Dream (1989)
Stunts (1989)
Graystone Bag (1989)
Fire Mask (1990)
Something Stirs (1991)
Raven (1993)
Jackals (1994)
Watcher (1997)

Millennium Quartet

Symphony (1997)
In the Mood (1998)
Chariot (1999)
Riders in the Sky (1999)

Black Oak Series

Genesis (1998)
Hugh of Dark Wings (1999)
Winter Knight (1999)
Hunting Ground (2000)
When the Cold Wind Blows (2001)

Oxrun Series

The Hour of the Oxrun Dead (1977)
The Sound of Midnight (1978)
Grave (1979)
The Last Call of Morning (1979)
The Soft Whisper of the Dead (1982)
The Blood Wind (1982)
Nightmare Seasons (1982)
The Dark Cry of the Moon (1985)
The Long Night of the Grave (1986)
The Orchard (1987)
Dialing the Wind (1989)

Paric Series

The Shadow of Alpha (1976)
Ascension (1977)
Legion (1979)

X-File Novels

Goblins (1994)
Whirlwind (1995)

COLLECTIONS

Tales from the Nightside (1981)
A Glow of Candles (1981)
Midnight (1985)
The Black Carousel (1995)
A Quiet Way to Scream (1996)
Gothic Ghosts (1997)

(Written as Felicia Andrews)

Mountainwitch (1980)
Moon Witch (1980)

(Written as Lionel Fen)

The Seven Spears of the W'dch'ck (1998)
Once Upon a Time in the East (1993)
By the Time I Get to Nashville (1994)
Time: The Semi-Final Frontier (1994)
Blood River Down (1986)
Web of Defeat (1987)
Agnes Day (1987)

(Written as Kent Montana)

Kent Montana and the Really Ugly Thing from Mars (1990)
Kent Montana and the Reasonably Invisible Man (1991)
Kent Montana and the Once and Future Thing (1991)
The Mark of the Moderately Vicious Vampire (1992)
668: The Neighbor of The Beast (1992)

(Written as Steve Charles)

Nightmare Session (1986)
Academy of Terror (1986)
Witch's Eye (1986)
Skeleton Key (1986)
The Enemy Within (1987)
The Last Alien (1987)

(Written as Geoffrey Marsh)

The King of Satan's Eyes (1984)
The Tale of the Arabian Knight (1986)
The Patch of the Odin Soldier (1987)
The Fangs of the Hooded Demon (1988)
Hudson Hawk (Novelization) (1991)

Awards

Nebula Award in 1976 for his short story "A Crowd of Shadows."
Nebula Award in 1978 for his novella "A Glow of Candles, a Unicorn's Eye."

World Fantasy Award for *Nightmare Seasons* (*novella*)
British Lifetime Achievement Award
Bram Stoker Lifetime Achievement Award
International Horror Guild's Living Legend

    Charles L. Grant also edited the award winning *Shadows* anthology, running eleven volumes from 1978 to 1991. Contributors include Stephen King, Ramsey Campbell, Al Sarrantonio, R.A. Lafferty, Avram Davidson, and Steve Rasnic and Melanie Tem.

    Grant was a former executive secretary and eastern regional director of the Science Fiction and Fantasy Writers of America and president of the Horror Writers Association.

"When I first started writing, I did two pages a day, five or six days a week. Why two pages? Because on my worst day I could do two pages before I had to get to work in corporate America. I was working a full-time job when I started my first book, so I know it's hard to fit it in, but not impossible. Some people prefer to work at night, but for me, after a full day's work, I could barely think, let alone be creative."

— *Laurell K. Hamilton*

Seduced by Moonlight: Laurell K. Hamilton

One of the top vampire writers in America, Laurell K. Hamilton burst onto the scene in 1993 with a paperback titled Guilty Pleasure, *which introduced the world to Anita Blake, a vampire hunter and animator of the recent dead.* Laughing Corpse *followed in 1994. For the rest of the decade and into the new millennium, her popularity rose with each new Anita Blake book. Her most recent is* Bullet, *her 20th Anita Blake novel.*

Hamilton began a very different fantasy series with her Meredith Gentry books in 2000. She started with Kiss of Shadows, *which was about the faerie princess of the Unseelie Court, and continued with* Caress of Twilight. *She is currently working on her third installment,* Seduced by Moonlight.

Hamilton lives in St. Louis with her family and is active in animal charities. Her Web site is laurellkhamilton.com.

In the *Anita Blake: Vampire Hunter* series, you created a world where vampires, zombies and werewolves inhabit the United States and have legal status. How did you invent this imaginative universe?

Anita's world is based on ours. As if we went to bed tonight, and when we woke up tomorrow, vampires, zombies, ghouls, werewolves, everything that goes bump in the night, were real. And the modern world had to deal with them, bang. I wanted to play in modern America with the addition of monsters with folklore and mythology. Where the desire came from, I no longer remember. Probably I couldn't have told you at the time. Not exactly. Ideas are like that sometimes.

If they were real, what night club would you rather go to — the Laughing Corpse or Narcissus in Chains?

Narcissus in Chains, I guess; though, naughty you, only giving me two choices.

Okay, let me rephrase that. If you could go to any club in Anita Blake's world, where would you go?

Danse Macabre if I was going out for an evening with my husband. Burnt Offerings if I was doing a family night out.

How do you keep the subject matter fresh for yourself? Is there a fear you'd run out of ideas for future novels?

After, or maybe before, I finished *Guilty Pleasures*, the first Anita book, I had tentative plots for some fifteen or seventeen more books. I've still not gotten even halfway through the list, because the books I've written have birthed new ideas, new characters, and taken the series in directions I never dreamt. New book ideas keep coming because Anita's world is so fresh, alive, real, in the way that the best fictional worlds can be.

How long do you plan on continuing the Meredith Gentry series?

Indefinitely. It's like a mystery series with no set limit or ending. Merry was set up to have a happy-ever-after ending. Somewhere between book seven and book twelve the story will be over. Merry will have her storybook ending. It is a fairy tale, after all.

The creator and author of the Anita Blake and Merry Gentry books, Laurell K. Hamilton (photograph by Stefan Hester, 2009).

Of all the novels you have written, what are your top favorite three and why?

It's like asking someone to pick their favorite child. I just can't do it.

Meredith Gentry shares your grandmother's surname. Was there a reason for this?

When I was in elementary school, I learned that Gentry could mean blue-blood [noble], or be a polite euphemism for the fey, the little people. I loved the idea that my family name could mean we were descended from fairies. It amused me then, and apparently it still does. Other than that, it has no bearing on my family, or my grandmother.

Was *Circus of the Damned* inspired by the Hammer movie *Vampire Circus*?

Yes and no. I think that my vampires in general were influenced by my being allowed to watch the Hammer vampire films. *Vampire Circus* was one of those movies. The vamp at the beginning with the frilly white shirt and long dark hair reminds me of Jean-Claude. I was probably seven when I saw the movie. A movie that includes a vampire that changes form into a black leopard. I certainly think it left its mark on my subconscious, but *Circus of the Damned* was not based on the movie.

Early in your career, you wrote a *Star Trek* media tie-in book, *Star Trek: The Next Generation: Night Shade #24*. How much freedom did you have to work in a universe that was already created and very popular?

I knew going in that I was playing in someone else's sandbox, with someone else's toys. I actually had more freedom to play than I thought I would. My biggest surprise came when the editor sent the first draft back and told me I could torture Captain Picard. He had not been tortured on the television show at that time. I replied, "I can torture Picard, really?" They said, "Yes, as long as it is a clean and futuristic torture. No blood and guts." Okay. I enjoyed the experience.

Were you worried about your writing future when your first book, *Nightseer*, was only moderately successful?

Yes. If I'd been easily discouraged, I could have been a one-hit wonder.

How do you feel about the Anita Blake–"Buffy the Vampire Slayer" comparisons?

I'm fine with it.

Have the Anita Blake or Meredith Gentry novels sparked interest from Hollywood?

Some, nothing definite.

What was the first horror or science fiction story you remember reading that had an impact on you?

Robert E. Howard's short story "Pigeons from Hell."

Dark sexuality is an element that runs through your books. Why is this? And does it shock you sometimes?

One of the things that puzzled me in most horror novels was the level of punishment for sex. Sex of almost any kind either caused horrible things to happen, or was punished by death, or possession, or other terrible things. I never understood why this Puritan attitude towards sex seemed so prevalent in a genre that prided itself on pushing almost every other kind of boundary. I mean, I'd read books that were so graphic in their violence that it made me queasy, yet put a little sex in and everything goes to hell. This seemed a backwards kind of thinking. Shouldn't violence be a worse crime than sex? I did not purposely set out to be the spokesperson for fictional sexual freedom, but it seems to have turned out that way. There was a time when sex embarrassed me, but not shocked, no.

What draws you to vampires as characters?

I don't really know. Maybe I'm just orally fixated. Remember, I write about shapeshifters, too, and they get to do more than just drink blood.

Having written on the themes of vampires for almost a decade now, have you noticed any significant changes in your writing style?

My writing has changed a great deal, as any writer's will after a decade. My writing has become more lush, richer. I can be sparse and minimalistic when I want to be, or I can wrap the sensuality of the words across the paper. It's a choice now, rather than a happy accident.

Any advice for beginning writers?

First, a writer writes. I've lost track of the number of people who want to be writers but never actually write anything. Talking about writing, dreaming about writing, can be very fun, but it won't get a book written. You've got to write, so that when the o'clock rolls around you feel almost compelled to sit down and write something; or have a page quotient because if you finish your pages early you get to get up and do something else. Of course, the reverse is true: If you don't get your pages accomplished, you can be sitting at your desk for a very long time.

When I first started writing, I did two pages a day, five or six days a week. Why two pages? Because on my worst day I could do two pages before I had to get to work in corporate America. I was working a full-time job when I started my first book, so I know it's hard to fit it in, but not impossible. Some people prefer to work at night, but for me, after a full day's work, I could barely think, let alone be creative. I had to work first thing in the morning or I wouldn't have written anything. By the way, I am not a morning person. I got up, stumbled out of bed and sat at the computer until I had those two pages, then I got dressed and went to play executive.

Here's the secret to finishing that first book. Don't rewrite as you go. Let me repeat that one. Don't rewrite as you go along. I know one writer who has three wonderful first chapters of a book. They are wonderful, and they should be. He's been rewriting them for about nine years now. He wanted the beginning to be perfect before he moved on. He's never going to finish the book, because perfectionism is an unattainable goal. It isn't going to be perfect. Just get words down on paper, and when you stumble to what you think is the end of the book, you have hundreds of pages of words that came out of your head. It may not be perfect, but it looks like a book, or rather a book manuscript.

Books by Laurell K. Hamilton

NOVELS

Nightseer (1992)
Star Trek: The Next Generation: Night Shade #24 (1992)
Ravenloft: Death of the Dark Lord (1995)

ANITA BLAKE SERIES

Guilty Pleasure (1993)
Laughing Corpse (1994)
Circus of the Damned (1995)
The Lunatic Cafe (1996)
Bloody Bones (1996)
The Killing Dance (1997)
Burnt Offerings (1998)
Blue Moon (1998)
Obsidian Butterfly (2000)
Narcissus in Chains (2001)
Cerulean Sin (2003)
Incubus Dreams (2005)
Micah (2006)
Danse Macabre (2006)
Strange Candy (2006)
The Harlequin (2007)
Blood Noir (2008)
Skin Trade (2009)
Flirt (2010)
Bullet (2010)

Meredith Gentry Books

Kiss of Shadows (2000)
Caress of Twilight (2002)
Seduced by Moonlight (2004)
A Stroke of Midnight (2005)
Mistral's Kiss (2006)
A Lick of Frost (2007)
Swallowing Darkness (2008)
Divine Misdemeanor (2009)

Other Books

Out of This World by J.D. Robb (2001)
    Also with Laurell K. Hamilton, Susan Krinard and Maggie Shaune
Craving (2004)
    Also with MaryJanice Davidson, Eileen Wilks and Rebecca York
Bite (2005)
    Also with Charlaine Harris, MaryJanice Davidson, Angela Knight and Vickie Taylor
Never After (2009)
    Also with Yasmine Galenorn and Majorie M. Liu

Awards

P.E.A.R.L. (Paranormal Excellence Award for Romantic Literature) for *A Kiss of Shadows* 2000

"Writing is my passion. I believe my legacy will be as a publisher of Ray Bradbury and Richard Matheson. Fifty years after I'm gone, I know there will be those reading our books by Bradbury and Matheson that no mass market publisher would touch and it will brighten their day. And, as scholars put these two wonderful authors and men in perspective, our books will be part of the foundation for their analysis. Still, given a choice, my own writing speaks for me and makes me even more aware how difficult it is to achieve what authors like Bradbury and Matheson have."

— *Barry Hoffman*

Guardian of Lost Souls: Barry Hoffman
by Michael McCarty and Mark McLaughlin

Most people are happy if they have one major career going for them. Barry Hoffman is one of those rare and fortunate people who have the drive and vision to excel in multiple careers—in his case, three. In his life, he has been a teacher, a writer and a publisher. Even though he is now retired from teaching, he is still an educator: His magazine Gauntlet *informs readers about the perils of censorship.*

Barry also publishes limited edition collectible books under the Gauntlet imprint. His authors, past and present, are a publisher's dream team: literary icons like Ray Bradbury, Richard Matheson, William F. Nolan, F. Paul Wilson, and Robert Bloch, to name just a few. He also produces the Edge Books line of trade paperbacks.

Barry also writes fiction, including the Eyes *series of novels (*Hungry Eyes, Eyes of Prey, Judas Eyes, Blindsided, *and* Blind Vengeance*); the stand-alone novel* Born Bad; *young adult books; and the fiction collections* Guardian of Lost Souls *and* Love Hurts. *His fiction has appeared in such high-profile anthologies as* The Earth Strikes Back, Return to the Twilight Zone *and* Werewolves.

Let's talk about your early influences. Can you remember the first scary book you ever read, or the first scary movie you ever saw?

I'm not good at firsts, but I was a big moviegoer so I know it was a movie that had the biggest impact on me. I believe it was *The Blob* that scared the crap out of me. Something that could devour others (me!!!) was pretty terrifying.

As a publisher, you've worked with some big names, including Bradbury and Matheson. How did you start working with them?

I first communicated with Ray Bradbury while teaching. My students would read some of his classic short stories and critique them. I'd found out his address and sent him my students' work. While he couldn't respond to each and every critique individually, he wrote back a wonderful letter and signed a poster which went right up on a bulletin board in my classroom. One thing I learned early with Bloch, Bradbury and Matheson was that unlike many authors, *none* of them had a staff who answered their mail. Each read all mail received and responded. Bloch once sent me a handwritten letter, apologizing that his typewriter was in the shop being fixed. He was sending me the introduction to *Psycho*.

Head of the class. Barry Hoffman at Springs Ranch Elementary School, Colorado Springs, Colorado (photograph by Dara Hoffman, 2009).

Bloch was actually the connection between all three. I approached Bradbury and Matheson to write an introduction and afterword to our classic-revisited of *Psycho*. Both wrote these wonderful moving pieces that talked about Bloch the author and Bloch the "gentleman." When I saw how few books by Matheson and Bradbury had been published as signed limiteds, I approached both. Bradbury immediately agreed. Matheson was a bit more hesitant, possibly because he had been burned by Dream/Press who never paid him for the signed limited of his collected stories. He had three "demands." He wouldn't write an introduction to his books (this changed after we began working together). I asked if he would agree to an interview which would be turned into an introduction. He agreed … reluctantly. Next, he couldn't sign tipsheets in a short period of time. I said we would send them to him six months in advance. He agreed … reluctantly. Last, if we wanted someone to write an intro or afterword, we would have to approach them (he relented on this, too, later, suggesting and even contacting others on our behalf). Not a problem, I told him. He then agreed … reluctantly, and not too soon after *He Is Legend* was published. There was no reluctance after that.

Is the market for collectible books getting better or worse?

I know some publishers are decrying the current market due to the economy and I won't disagree. You have collectors getting married and starting families. Well, you can't start a family and collect signed limited editions. Not unless you're already rich. And, I know some collectors have to give up their passion when they purchase a house and all of a sudden have a mortgage. But … all of our recent Repairman Jack books have sold out on publication. Keep in mind that these same people could wait three to four months for a less expensive trade edition of the book. The lettered and numbered editions of *He Is Legend* sold out in about a week and I have a long waiting list for both editions. So, I think if there are good books out there, they will sell regardless of the economy.

I do think collectors are becoming more discriminating. They have just so-much money so they can't splurge as they did ten or twenty years ago. And some customers get a sour taste in their mouths when a publisher goes belly-up with customers' money in their pockets or they don't publish a book for three or more years. This has happened before and it takes a long time for people to trust the specialty press again. Without mentioning any names, it's happening again now and it could hurt *all* specialty presses.

That's why at Gauntlet we don't take a penny until the year the book is to be published. We publish on time so customers know they won't have to wait years for a book they've paid for. But, some prospective customers, who haven't dealt with us before, are wary because of bad experiences they've had. There will always be a market for collectibles. Just like mass market publishers (who are making severe cuts), the specialty press has to treat their business as a business so they can publish during the bad times, so as to prosper during the good times.

Which came first: Barry the writer or Barry the publisher?

Definitely the writer. I was sometimes pretty miserable at the school (I was the individualist where conformity was beginning to be demanded), and

I took out my frustrations on paper. I wrote one short story that was pretty pitiful and I don't even have a copy of it. In it, a teacher (me, with a different name) jiggered with the electricity so that when the principal came to his room and turned on the light, he got fried. I also told my students stories. When I gave a spelling test I'd tell a story, off the top of my head. There was a girl in one of my classes, Marjorie, who spent the entire day combing her hair. I'd tell her to stop and ten minutes later she was at it again. I told her one day if she continued, I'd write a story about it for the class to read. She didn't believe me — even dared me to write it with a "No you won't" — so I wrote "Lice." Not a great story either, but the class enjoyed it. Marjorie enjoyed it. She was the center of attention even if she did meet with a terrible end. My passion has always been writing and immersing myself into my characters.

How did you go from a teacher to a publisher?

Simply put, I was censored by my principal which both provided me time to publish and a cause to champion. I first published *Gauntlet* magazine which dealt with censorship. The genesis of the magazine were plays I wrote for my middle school students to perform. I wrote plays on the homeless, on being an outcast, runaways and drug abuse, among others. We had a professional composer write original songs featuring lyrics my students wrote, and a professional choreographer worked with my students on dance numbers. The head of the school PTA (in Philly it was called the Home and School Association) didn't like some of the lyrics of one of the songs: a runaway had "sex" and contracted AIDS. We had to delete the word "sex" for something tamer. Then my principal line-edited the play. What was both ironic and pitiful was that he accused me of using "black" dialogue — sentences that were grammatically incorrect — and he demanded changes. The character in question was based on a *white* janitor. The speech patterns had nothing to do with race and all to do with economics.

In any event, I wasn't invited to write a play the following year, even though all of our plays were sold-out SRO affairs and we'd received critical acclaim from local newspapers and TV stations. All of a sudden I literally had hundreds of free hours. I'd been a fan of genre magazines and thought I could do as well as those being published. So, I had a desire to publish a magazine and now an issue — censorship.

My students had communicated with Ray Bradbury (critiquing his short stories which I had them read) and when I asked if he would allow me to publish some of his work in *Gauntlet* he agreed. With Bradbury on board, it wasn't difficult to attract other big genre names. That was in 1990–91. Fast forward one years and having published several issues of the magazine, I felt

I could do an equally good job publishing books, especially from authors whose work I loved, who influenced my own writing and whose work I'd had my students read in class. Our second book was Bob Bloch's *Psycho*. With many mid-list authors having expensive signed limiteds published, I was shocked that *Psycho* had never been given that treatment. Bloch readily agreed and when I asked who should write the intro and afterword he said he wasn't worthy to make a suggestion. I knew that both Richard Matheson and Ray Bradbury were great fans of Bloch's work and good friends of his. I contacted them and both not only agreed to take part but wrote wonderful pieces. They did so not knowing that Bloch had contracted terminal cancer.

His death made me change the focus of my publishing. Again, I was flabbergasted at how few of both Matheson's and Bradbury's classics had been published as signed limiteds. Starting in 1993, I believe, I've published at least one Bradbury and Matheson book per year; first their classics and later their unpublished work. All because my fool principal was a racist and censored my writing.

I've always been a reader, whether it be nonfiction or the works of authors in a variety of genres. Books became even more important when I began teaching and saw the poor quality of writing my students were forced to read in "basal" readers. I would prowl used bookstores for books of short stories by Matheson, Bradbury, King, Edgar Allan Poe, Rod Serling's stories he wrote based on scripts from *The Twilight Zone*, Henry Slesar (an underappreciated writer), Shirley Jackson and many others. My principal wasn't very happy that I deviated from the curriculum. (A common theme — my alienating my principal. I spent as much time in his office as some of my wayward students.) But he grudgingly allowed me to continue. So, yes, books have always been important to me, and introducing my students to these wonderful writers, one of my greatest achievements as a teacher.

You've published the works of Bloch, Matheson, Bradbury, Poppy Z. Brite, William Nolan and Jack Ketchum. Is there anyone on your dream list you haven't published yet, that you would like to publish?

I would have loved to have published Jack Finney's *Invasion of the Body Snatchers*. Sadly he passed away just as I began to publish books. I'm publishing an anthology with a short story collaboration between Stephen King and his son Joe Hill so I am publishing Stephen King. I'd love to publish David Morrell (he has written an introduction for one of our Matheson books). I've had discussions with him but we just haven't found anything yet. I consider him one of the best pure writers on the planet. I read his books and learn something about writing that I try to use in my books. He approaches a chase scene like nobody else, for instance. I'd love to gain access to the archives of Shirley Jackson to see if there are alternate versions of "The Lottery." Her estate has not been responsive to my requests. And, looking back even further, I wonder if there are early versions of some of Poe's stories.

What do you consider Gauntlet Press' greatest achievement?

Our greatest achievement has been to publish previously unpublished material by some of the masters. We published Richard Matheson's first novel, *Hunger and Thirst*. When he hadn't sold it as a young man he put it away, along with many other great works. We published a number of his scripts which, for varying reasons, were never produced. And, in 2007 we published his script for *I Am Legend*, which ironically had been censored by the British and American Film Boards. Those who have seen any of the [movie] adaptations of his classic novel (there have been three with the most recent, the Will Smith blockbuster) haven't seen a true adaptation of *I Am Legend*. Matheson's written it and hopefully one day a film will be made based on his script. We've done the same with Bradbury. *Dark Carnival*, which Bradbury initially didn't want republished, is one of our greatest achievements. We added five stories (all unpublished) that he wanted in the book but Arkham House couldn't include due to space limitations. And our most enduring book I think will be *Match to Flame* which includes all of Bradbury's fiction that influenced and led up to his classic *Fahrenheit 451*.

Why did you start Edge Books?

Edge Books is our trade paperback line. Other publishers had published a limited edition of both Matheson's *Twilight Zone* scripts and his collected short stories. I wanted to provide these wonderful books to the general public. TOR yearly releases a dozen or so of Matheson's short stories (usually the best known) and charges a small fortune for them. We published 99 of Matheson's short stories in three volumes. Our promise was to keep them in print as long as we remained in business. We've fulfilled that goal. We've done the same with Poppy Z. Brite and Jack Ketchum. To date we've sold out 10,000 copies of Poppy's *Are You Loathsome Tonight?* It's a book no mass market publisher was willing to publish. So, we've provided a huge service to her fans.

You are currently working on your sixth *Eyes* book. What can you tell us about it?

Since the fifth book is still awaiting publication I don't want to spoil that read by telling too much about the sixth book, but basically it is the end of the series, yet, hopefully the beginning of another. With the sixth book I believe I've plunged the depths of Shara Farris, the main character, as far as I can. I only decided to follow *Hungry Eyes* with a second, then a third and fourth book because I felt the need to further develop Shara's character. In the sixth book, one of the other characters, who has been of great significance to Shara, shares center stage with Shara. So, the series can continue, in a manner of speaking, with this other character taking center stage. The sixth book will also contain a novella in which this new main character steps out on her own to investigate a mysterious death.

Being the publisher-editor of Gauntlet Press must keep you busy. Who are the other staffers at your publishing house?

In many respects, Gauntlet Press is a one-man show. My daughter is now layout editor. She designs all but one book each year and has done a fabulous job. She is also in charge of our website and newsletter. I do all the glamourous chores like sending out invoices, packing and shipping books, processing orders, entering them into the database and responding to calls and emails. I'd love to hand them off to someone else, but I'm a bit paranoid. What would happen if a dozen customers didn't get their order, for instance? So, I guess I've been afraid to hand these chores off.

What I find most gratifying is working hands-on with each title. I often ask authors for additional material to go into our lettered editions (for the money someone is paying for a lettered edition, I believe the customer should get more than a traycase and additional piece of art). With our Rod Serling script series, for instance, for each of the five volumes (there will be ten in all) we've published, in the lettered edition there is an added script — a variation on one of the scripts in the book that is often far different [from] Serling's final shooting script.

Harry O. Morris is pretty much our in-house artist. Harry's a wonderful artist who is no one-trick pony. He has numerous styles and the authors I publish seem to love working with him. Matheson won't work with any other artist. Harry has worked with F. Paul Wilson on all of the Repairman Jack books we've published. And, recently, he has become a favorite of Jack Ketchum. He's also done the cover art for all of my books; some really visceral pieces that are far different than anything he's done for other authors. My son is my West Coast staffer. He scans material we need and is my main contact with both Matheson and Bradbury. I really envy him. He brings tipsheets over to Bradbury and while Bradbury signs them he spins yarns to my son.

The cover for *Eyes of Prey* is so evocative and emotional at the same time...

That was Harry Morris. Oddly, that wasn't going to be the cover. Harry and I discussed a cover and he did a wonderful job on it (it's the endpaper of the lettered edition of the book). For an interior illustration I told him to do whatever he wanted, as long as it was visceral. When I saw the piece (a girl in the shower who had been raped and is trying to wash the rapist off of her),

I had to give Harry both the good and bad news. He readily agreed that that second piece would be the cover art. I spend a full chapter dealing with the trauma this character experienced as a result of her rape. Harry conveyed the same with his illustration. He's that talented. We also used the piece as cover art for one of the issues of *Gauntlet* magazine dealing with erotic art.

Your books can be very violent. Was it hard to shift gears to write the young adult book *Curse of the Shamra*?

First, while there is violence in my book, it is more implied violence than the blood and gore variety. My feeling is that if you are going to do blood and gore, you have to do it well. Jack Ketchum does it well. The late Richard Laymon did it well. Many authors can't pull it off. [For authors who] get stuck with the plot, slice and dice someone because that's the easy way out. So, rather than spilling gallons of blood, I spend far more time on character — often the traumas of those who populate my books.

Many of my characters are neither good nor evil, but dwell on a line where a gentle push one way or another can make them heroic or the villain. Think of cops. There are many who cross that line. Most cops start out as virtuous. However, some take a bribe, then another, and soon they are corrupt. Others use their authority to the extreme. They live in a violent world and often commit violent acts that if they weren't cops they would be imprisoned for. My characters are those shades of gray; some decent people who go wrong and others who don't cross over to the dark side.

Anyway, back to your question. It wasn't difficult at all to shift gears for *Curse of the Shamra*. If you're writing a book for young adults, there are some things you can't do or the books won't get into schools. My characters in the book don't curse. There is no sex and the violence is implied. However, I don't write down to those readers. Adults can enjoy the book as well as teens. The main character isn't much different from Shara from the *Eyes* series or other characters I've created. She's conflicted. She's a female in a society where females are supposed to be submissive [but she] refuses to be the "good female." She gets her chance to lead a resistance movement and learns that being a leader is far more difficult than she thought. She makes errors of judgment. She sometimes lets her emotions get the best of her. But when called upon to lead, she accepts the challenge and all the baggage that comes with leadership.

Tell us about the unpublished Ray Bradbury novel *Masks* that your house will be releasing.

Masks is Donn Albright's baby. I get the feeling speaking with him that this might be one of Donn's favorite pieces of Bradbury's writing. Bradbury began *Masks* when he was quite young and dirt poor. He wrote an outline in narrative form that was the basis for a Guggenheim grant he applied for. He didn't get the grant. *Masks* basically deals with the many faces and personalities people adopt. In this case the main character lost himself in multiple personalities. Bradbury never completed the novel, but for the next six or seven years worked on it periodically. ([He did the same thing] with *Somewhere a Band Is Playing* which he did finish after fifty years. Both we and HarperCollins published the novella, but we added fragments which showed the different directions Bradbury was considering.) Donn has put these fragments for *Masks* together to form a coherent story. And, as an added bonus, he got permission from Bradbury to include a number of other stories written around the same time that had never been published. They all deal with themes covered in *Masks*. What you have is a new Bradbury collection with *Masks* as the centerpiece.

The Richard Matheson Companion is an incredibly detailed book, a real tribute to Matheson. Are you planning any other books like that?

Not at the moment. There's already a *Bradbury Companion* and to be perfectly honest, I think that only the cream of the crop of authors deserve such books. A *Robert Bloch Companion* would be interesting, but you have to find the right editor for such a project. That's no easy chore. Right now I'm more interested in publishing some of Matheson's uncollected works — both short stories and some aborted novels. Volume 1, coming out this summer [20xx], includes his one *Star Trek* script, "The Enemy Within." And, I'm having a ball with Ray Bradbury's unpublished material. Donn has supplied stories, scripts and fragments, on *Masks* which will be out this Halloween and a second *Bullet Trick* (both teleplays and short stories) which is a 2010 project.

Speaking of Matheson, what can you tell us about the *He is Legend* anthology?

It's an incredible book. Christopher Conlon came to me with the idea. My primary objective in anything I do with Matheson is to respect the man and his work. Before I would agree to the project, I spoke to Matheson. He was flattered and gave his approval. Harry Morris, once again, did the artwork. Then it was a matter of making sure the book included material from some of the best writers of the genre since this was a tribute book to Matheson. I was really excited that authors like F. Paul Wilson, Joe Lansdale, Whitley Strieber and R.C. Matheson were interested. Then Nancy Collins and Joe Hill came on board. I contacted King, on behalf of the Matheson family, and he wanted to write a collaboration with his son. And to top it off, we have a collaboration between Matheson and the late Charles Beaumont, *Conjure Wife*. Again, another unpublished script that will only add to the legacy of both authors.

How did *Match to Flame: The Fictional Paths to Fahrenheit 451* get started?

That was my baby, at least the idea. I'd wanted to publish a limited edition of *Fahrenheit 451*. It's probably the only work by Bradbury I wanted to publish but hadn't. Two other publishers (one a library) published limited editions. Neither did the book justice. They were basically signed reprints which I find shameful. I know what I would have added if we had done the book. But, we ended up doing the next best thing, collecting stories and novellas (both published and unpublished) that traced in fiction the path to *Fahrenheit 451*. Donn was a godsend for the project. He had two unpublished and incomplete novellas Bradbury had tinkered with that contained ideas that would become part of *Fahrenheit 451*.

One, "Ignorant Armies," was typical Bradbury, as far as his writing was concerned. Bradbury would have an idea and over a period of years tinker with it. A fragment of four to five pages here and another fragment of the same length there. You put them all together and you get a coherent story. Sometimes (like with *Somewhere a Band Is Playing*) he would complete the novel-novella and it would see publication. Other times he just put it away. Donn organized a massive amount of fragments to form a coherent novella for "Ignorant Armies." What I enjoyed so much was seeing how Bradbury tinkered with the idea. For instance, the character who would become Montag had a number of other names in the novella. Bradbury started with one name, changed it and then later returned to the original name; none Montag. It's incredible to see how he played with different elements of the novella. It opens a door into the mind of one of our greatest authors that's truly fascinating. And some of the stories in the book are far bleaker than *Fahrenheit 451*. To see the metamorphosis of these stories into *Fahrenheit 451* was incredible.

As more people turn to the Internet for entertainment needs, will books still be valued in the years to come?

There will always be those who want (even need) to feel a real book in order to read it. Keep in mind that when books came out on tape (now they're on CDs), the same question was asked. You don't get the same experience reading a book on the Internet or a machine you can carry with you. When I take my granddaughter to a swimming pool or go on an airplane, a majority of the passengers are still reading the old-fashioned way — a book.

Are any of your novels being considered for movie production?

None at the moment. *Hungry Eyes* has been optioned but nothing came of it. I know a number of authors whose work has been purchased and ten years later there still is no movie. It's Hollywood at its worst. Look at the script used for the Will Smith *I Am Legend*. It went through any number of drafts and as a result it stunk. There was already a phenomenal script written by Matheson himself. A real shame. That's one reason you have so few memorable movies each season. On the other hand there are far fewer restrictions for television. You can't wait two to three years to get the script you want for the next episode of a series. That's why a show like *Lost* is so great. A small group of writers take care of the entire series. Some of the best written scripts are now being written for television which many films flounder under the weight of rewrites.

Which of your novels would make the best films?

I'd have to say *Born Bad*. The villain in *Born Bad* may be my favorite character and I think moviegoers would enjoy all the mischief she creates without getting caught. Shanicha is also a complex character with demons of her own. When my son read the book (I encouraged my children to read my books even when they were young), Shanicha was not only his favorite character, but he sympathized with her to some extent. That validated the character to me. What Shanicha does is often truly heinous so to be able to feel sympathetic to her means I succeeded in creating an interesting character.

The topic of censorship is a major theme with your magazine *Gauntlet*. How does America compare with other countries on the issue of censorship? How free is the land of the free?

While there is still a good deal of censorship here, it pales in comparison to the rest of the world. In far too many countries, what can and can't be read is strictly regulated. I've read how in China, the Internet is sometimes blocked (don't ask me how) so the Chinese can't read about the oppression they suffer. In many countries, newspapers are regulated by the government. I just heard today that some newspapers in Iraq who were critical of the government were shut down — and our soldiers are dying for this government. Journalists in foreign countries have been imprisoned. So, compared to other countries, we are an oasis in the desert.

But, that doesn't mean everything's the way it should be here. Most damaging are special interest groups who don't want the cause they espouse to be criticized. They do their worst at the local level, joining and even leading library committees and school boards where they decide what can be allowed to be read and what is banned. Books dealing with alternative lifestyles are routinely censored in many communities and it doesn't make headlines. Sex education in many areas is ludicrous with abstinence-only classes offered in too many locales. Blacks, Hispanics, Muslims, gays and anti-gays, evangelists, the blind and every other special interest group has advocacy groups that want their group viewed in only positive terms, and picket or file frivolous lawsuits to protect their special interest. It's censorship of the worst kind. At the same time, the Internet offers an enormous amount of uncensored material which, for the most part, can't be regulated. However, a word of caution. You can bet that these special interests groups are trying to find ways to censor and/or control the Internet. I would bet against them succeeding.

Do you attend mystery or horror conventions?

When I lived back East, prior to 2002, I attended a number of cons. I'd go to Chiller with Jack Ketchum and we'd have a ball. I regularly attended Horrorfind. Sadly, from what I hear, writers are getting pushed aside in favor of film personalities. I also went to at least five Necon cons which is probably the best "non-convention" that exists. It's held on a college campus and authors and fans mix — and drink and drink and drink some more. Fans get to meet authors in an informal setting and writers get time to swap war stories and ideas. I went to the Horror Writers Association meeting in New York City a few times. Since I moved to Colorado, though, I've found that attending conventions is a bit too expensive. I wish the World Horror Convention would return to Denver.

Talking about conventions, is true that you were once trapped in an elevator with Rain Graves and Brian Keene [Bram Stoker award–winning authors] and others at a horror con?

Oh yes. At Horrorfind. I believe it was the second year of Horrorfind. Far more people attended than were expected and the hotel was overwhelmed. Brian, Rain and a dozen or so others were in the elevator when it just stopped. No problem, right. Someone would notice. Well, it took a good while — at least half an hour — before anyone noticed. There were some people who began panicking. It was pretty claustrophobic. And, it was one of those elevators with a glass window so you could see outside. It was like, there are all those people walking around, yet nobody knew we were trapped. Then someone pulled out a cell phone and things got really comical. He or she called the hotel telling them we were trapped. At first we weren't believed. At some point, though, someone from the hotel decided to investigate and sure enough they found out we *were* trapped.

The fire department was called — we could see the fire truck from the window — and they pried the door open. Nobody was injured, though at least one person was treated [for] panic or claustrophobia. The rest of us went off to various parties.

It's easy to see that being a publisher can help your writing career by giving you a better grasp of what editors want. Is there any downside?

The downside is, if you do your job as a publisher, you don't have as much time as you'd like for your writing. At one time I was teaching and publishing *Gauntlet* magazine and books at the same time. I didn't know it at the time but I was working two full-time jobs. When I left the teaching profession, I found that publishing still took up much of my day.

What projects are on the horizon?

I've written a second and third young adult book that would complete the Shamra series. I came up with a new villain who appears in the second and third books — one that is far more insidious than the villains in *Curse of the Shamra*. I'm working on a Shanicha prequel because the character kept tugging at me. And, I've done a lot of research on a female *Lord of the Flies* book. I just haven't had the time to begin that one, though much of it is plotted out. It's a bit of a daunting project. Lots of characters and a number of different directions that are tugging at me. I often get ideas, jot them down and then play with them to see if it can work as a short story, novella or even a novel. I have a story in *He Is Legend* based on his short story "The Disappearing Act." A mini-collection of short stories was published last year entitled *Love Hurts*.

As much as I love publishing, I am a writer at heart. Writing is my passion. I believe my legacy will be as a publisher of Bradbury and Matheson. Fifty years after I'm gone, I know there will be those reading our books by Bradbury and Matheson that no mass market publisher would touch and it will brighten their day. And, as scholars put these two wonderful authors and men in perspective, our books will be part of the foundation for their analysis. Still, given a choice, my own writing speaks for me and makes me even more aware how difficult it is to achieve what authors like Bradbury and Matheson have.

Books by Barry Hoffman

EYES SERIES

Hungry Eyes (1997)
Eyes of Prey (1998)
Judas Eyes (2001)

NOVELS

Firefly ... Burning Bright (1996)
The Disney Kiss (1998)
Born Bad (2000)

COLLECTIONS

Love Hurts (2006)

Awards

Gauntlet Press Bram Stoker Special Small press award, 1998
Winner of the 2003 Benjamin Franklin Award for Juvenile Fiction
Included on Fall 2002 Children's Book Sense 76 List
Bram Stoker for *He Is Legend: An Anthology Celebrating Richard Matheson* Anthology 2010

"My novels never work out exactly as I think they will, and that's sort of intentional. I don't outline, I simply begin when I have an interesting idea or image, when I'm burning to explore and see where it takes me. This usually leads to a lot of mess as I go. Sometimes pieces of scenes and dialogue get written that might get dropped in later in the novel. But there's never a tight structure that I work out ahead of time."

— *Nate Kenyon*

The Bone Factory: Nate Kenyon
by Michael McCarty and Mark McLaughlin

Nate Kenyon has been kicking at the door of the small press for the last few years with his creepy and cutting-edge short stories. His fiction has appeared in various magazines and the anthology Terminal Frights. *In January 2006 he became a full-fledged author when Five Star Books published his debut novel* Bloodstone, *which went on to become one of the publisher's all-time horror bestsellers, a P&E Award winner and a Bram Stoker Award finalist. Leisure Books released* Bloodstone *in paperback in 2008, and Kenyon's next novel* The Reach *later in the year. You can visit Nate online at www.natekenyon.com. This is what the Maine native (now a Bostonian) has to say.*

What was it like growing up in Maine?

Maine is a strange mix of cultures — those native to the state who are often struggling just to get by, and those who have moved in for various reasons, many of them searching for something. These two groups don't always blend particularly well. My parents were the hippie type, looking for a new frontier and a simpler life. My dad was a D.A. out in Seattle, my mother a schoolteacher, and one day they just decided to pull up roots and cross the country in a Volkswagen with two young children, all their belongings stuffed into the back. They rented a house in Richmond, and my father set up shop with a little law office while my mother learned to build houses. And that's exactly what she did, starting with ours; about a year later, we moved into this passive solar home she'd built with the help of her classmates on 60 acres of land.

I grew up on what might almost be considered a commune. But my parents were well-educated, liberal, and financially fairly well off, which didn't exactly fit the mold of a lot of my friends' families. My father was killed in a car accident when I was eight years old, and my mother got sick with cancer around that same time. These things all tended to isolate me, made me draw inward and feel like I was different from everyone else. I spent a lot of time during my early years exploring the woods around our home, reading, and writing stories. I got away from that by the time I entered high school and got into sports and girls and cars and all the normal things boys get into — but that tendency to daydream, to tell stories and escape into fiction, never completely left my blood.

I love Maine. It becomes a part of you, I think, and there's a real sense of loneliness up there, of vast, open space and very, very dark nights. It's very conducive to horror fiction. I hope to go back someday.

What is an average day in your life like?

Up at about 6:30 with our six-year-old climbing over me into the bed, digging her knobby knees and elbows into every single soft part of my anatomy before giving me a big sloppy kiss. Downstairs to make breakfasts and lunches for everyone, then once my wife and kids are out of the house, I have a few minutes to get ready for work. Then it's off to the office for my nine-to-five job as director of marketing and communications for the BC Law School. Most of my day is spent in meetings, or working on design and print projects. Sometimes I'm able to spend an hour at lunch working on new fiction, but usually I'm busy doing something related to the day job. At five I leave to pick up my daughter, and then it's home for dinner, playing with the kids and getting them to bed. After that, my wife and I open up our laptops and pound away at the keys until midnight. I'm either working on new projects, updating my website or surfing message boards like shocklines.com.

Weekends are reserved for house projects, writing and family time. If I'm on deadline for something, or finishing a novel, I'll pretty much lock myself away in the basement for a couple of days straight. A lot of people would think it's all sort of boring, I suppose, but I'm pretty happy. I hope someday to be able to write full-time, but until then, that's my routine.

There have been some comparisons of *The Reach* with Stephen King's *Firestarter*. How do you feel about that?

It's immensely flattering. I don't pretend to be operating at King's level, but if readers want to compare the two, that's fine with me. It was certainly an inspiration, along with many others. When I sat down to write *The Reach*, I had a very specific goal in mind: to write this type of story in the way Michael Crichton might have written it. I wanted to take the idea of telekinesis and write it like a techno-thriller — try to explain how it might actually occur from a scientific standpoint. So I did a lot of research to support the plot.

What was the inspiration for *The Bone Factory*?

The Bone Factory came right out of a vivid dream I had a few years ago. I woke up in the middle of the night with this image of a man, in the dead of winter and middle of the night, searching the woods alone for a dead body. It was an incredibly creepy dream and I got straight out of bed and wrote that first scene. Everything that came after grew from that.

***The Reach* has been optioned** for a major motion picture deal. Have any of your other books been?

The Reach is the first of my stories to be optioned for film. The company, PCH, is a relatively new outfit formed by a couple of long-time Hollywood producers, and they have quite a few movies under their belts. So I'm hopeful that this one will get made, although of course that's always a long shot, even at this stage. I'm just happy they saw enough in the story to want to option it.

What do you consider your best book published to date?

That's a tough question! It's like asking which of my children is my favorite. I suppose it would be between *The Reach* and *Prime*, my sci-fi novella. Both are (I think) my best writing, tightest plots, and have the most twists and turns. But I think the one coming in May 2010, *Sparrow Rock*, outdoes them both. It's my first first-person novel, it's my darkest, most intense work to date, and it contains some real shocking twists that I think are going to blow people away. After reading the draft, my editor called it a "modern classic of horror," which was a real thrill for me. I can't wait to get reader reactions to this one.

A review of *Bloodstone* stated that your portrayals of small-town lives and evils are dead-on. Other reviews have compared your work favorably to Stephen King, who often writes about small towns and is also from Maine. What is it about small-town New England life that inspired you to write horror about it?

Well, small-town life was certainly a part of my experience growing up.

There's a very interesting thing that happens in small towns: Even though you're nearest neighbor might be miles away, news travels fast. It's hard to keep a secret. Things tend to fester, too; old grudges, rumors, bad blood. I don't mean to make it sound terrible — there are a lot of good things about small towns too. But I think there's a certain type of evil that can fester in towns like White Falls, under the right circumstances.

Being compared to Stephen King is always a big thrill to me. I grew up idolizing his work, as many horror writers my age did, and he really opened my eyes to a new way of writing, fiction with an edge. His stuff was *nasty*. I loved it, and I wanted to do what he did. I think that it was after reading *The Shining* that I really thought about being a writer myself.

I do think small-town life in Maine is different than other places — the woods are deeper, the nights are darker, the wind blows cold and hard in the winter. It can feel very isolated, very desolate and lonely. You might live in the middle of town, and you might be able to see a neighbor's lights when you look out the window — but you know that on the other side of the house there are deep woods, and if something were to come out of there to get you, you'd never see it until it was too late.

Your novel *Bloodstone* follows the adventures of Billy Smith, an ex-con, and Angel, a prostitute and junkie. Would you consider these classic outsider characters?

I would consider them outsider characters, yes. Both of them have always struggled finding a place where they fit in. And that was a very intentional choice I made. It was all related to the story and what I was trying to do.

Do you consider yourself an outsider in any way?

For me personally, I've always felt sort of like two different people sharing one body. On the one hand, I'm a very sociable person — I like talking with people, and I love my family. People often describe me as friendly and outgoing. But there's another part of me that's always been shy and more introspective. As I described in an earlier answer, I went through a lot of trauma as a child, and I think that tended to make me more cautious when getting into more serious relationships. So in that way I might identify with Billy and Angel, even if most people who meet me might not realize it.

Of course, we know you didn't commit any crimes or do any streetwalking to research your book! But did you have to do any special research to learn how to portray the lives of an ex-con and a prostitute?

Don't be so sure! Actually, of the five or so manuscripts I've written so far, *Bloodstone* probably required the least amount of hard research. That's not to say I didn't do any; I knew about small-town life, and I knew people a lot like many of the characters in the book. Billy and Angel came to me pretty easily, although I did have to do a little digging about prison sentences and life behind bars. For the Thomas letters I had to learn what life was like in the 1700s. I also did some research on ancient cultures for some background to flesh out the plot.

Has anything supernatural or inexplicable ever happened to you?

Sure. I'm a pretty rational guy, really, but I think everyone has at least one or two experiences that might be considered odd. The first, and biggest, had to do with my father's death. I'd waited for him to come home from work as I always did, hiding in the closet so I could jump out at him and say, "Boo!" But that night, he didn't show, and after some frantic phone calls my mother found out he'd had an accident on the way home and was in the hospital. [There was] a flurry of activity — neighbors rushing to the house, my mother running out the door. I wanted to see him, but I was told that it wasn't a good time and that I could go see him in the morning. I was assured that he was just fine, nothing but a few scratches, and would be leaving the hospital in a few days.

I remember very clearly standing at the window in the kitchen as night fell. I stared out at the darkness and I knew he wasn't coming home. This was beyond simply being frightened of the unknown. I simply *knew*.

I told everyone that I had to go to the hospital. *I had to go.* I kicked and screamed about it. They tried to calm me down, and finally got me to sleep. The next morning I woke up and found my grandparents in the house. They told me my father had passed away in his sleep that night. I found out much later that although he'd been more severely injured than anyone told me — a broken rib, collapsed lung, and broken nose — he was expected to fully recover, and had been moved from intensive care. It was a freak blood clot that traveled to his other lung that had killed him. Nobody could have predicted it would happen.

How did you prepare for the challenge of writing your first novel?

I've written fiction my entire life. I remember a story I wrote when I was around eight years old called *The White Horse*. I made copies of it with carbon paper and sold it to my relatives for a quarter. I tried to write my first novel when I was a freshman in high school, and finished about fifty pages before giving up. It wasn't until I graduated from college that I made a serious commitment to write a complete novel, which I did while working at a law firm for the summer. Although there were definite highs and lows during the experience, and many times when I thought it was complete crap, I never really thought about not finishing it. It became a real challenge to me — write another ten pages, stack them up, and look at how many I had, then do it again. It was fun.

Have you written short stories?

Although I've written quite a bit of short fiction, I've always thought of myself as more of a novelist than a short story writer. Short stories are hard — every single word has to count, and the pacing must be just right. I find the novel form to be a lot easier.

Did *Bloodstone* develop exactly as you'd originally planned it, or did it change as you wrote it?

My novels never work out exactly as I think they will, and that's sort of intentional. I don't outline, I simply begin when I have an interesting idea or image, when I'm burning to explore and see where it takes me. This usually leads to a lot of mess as I go. Sometimes pieces of scenes and dialogue get written that might get dropped in later. But there's never a tight structure that I work out ahead of time.

That said, I do usually come up with major plot points and ideas that I jot down as the story progresses. For *Bloodstone*, I knew pretty early on that a couple of major events and plot twists were going to happen, so I was writing with them in mind. I guess you could say that the primary ideas in the book were there pretty much after the first couple of chapters, but a lot of character traits, minor events and other more specific things changed dramatically. Then it's all about the edits — going back through and refining the story, putting in more foreshadowing and streamlining the plot until it all makes sense.

How would you say the concepts of guilt and redemption fit into *Bloodstone*?

They're a major part of the theme. Guilt and the thought of redemption drive Billy Smith to do what he does. In many ways, *Bloodstone* is a quest novel, with Smith the flawed hero who is searching for redemption for what he did so many years ago. He's driven by his own guilt, but he's also driven by an internal desire to do what is right. One of the central ideas that fascinated me while writing this book was what exactly makes people react in such different ways to adversity. Why will one man rise up above difficult circumstances, while another will allow himself to be dragged down and destroyed? I set this premise up in the novel, with Billy and Jeb Taylor as mirror images of each other. One is driven to fight through the most difficult circumstances to do what is right, while the other cannot. I leave it up to the reader to decide why.

Who are your literary influences? What did you read, growing up?

I'd say King was my biggest influence, at least early on. But I read everything I could get my hands on as a child: mysteries, suspense, classics, horror, science fiction. I even read a few Danielle Steel and Sidney Sheldon novels that were lying around. I remember reading [James] Clavell's *King Rat* in fifth or sixth grade. I think I read my first King around then too. I still read everything I can. I think writers have to keep reading. It keeps the mind's mental connections going strong, and a love of the written word is essential.

Do you watch horror movies? What's your favorite?

Oh, sure. I love *The Silence of the Lambs, The Exorcist, Nightmare on Elm Street, Session 9, Jaws, The Shining*, and lots of others. I don't know if I could rank them. I was a huge slasher flick fan in high school. I was always the one trying to convince my friends to go to that B-horror movie playing at the local theater. These days, I really like the strong, atmospheric horror that gets you with slow building suspense and creepy settings. *Session 9* is a great example of that.

No bloodstone left unturned: Nate Kenyon outside of his office in Boston, Massachusetts (photograph by Harrison Malec-Brown, 2007).

You have a robust website—www.natekenyon.com. How has the Internet helped your writing career?

It's been a *huge* help to me. I was trying hard to break through for several years after college, back in the early '90s, and I really got burned out from all of that and left the genre for a while. When I started getting back into it last year and landed the contract for *Bloodstone*, I was amazed at the vibrant, thriving online community that had sprouted up while I was gone. It's so much easier these days to make connections through the web. It's opened up all sorts of new ways to promote my work message boards, online communities like MySpace, and of course my website. And the friendships I've made are wonderful. I'm a very big believer in the power of technology to transform the way we all work and live. I think we're only at the beginning of a revolution.

Do you plan on writing a sequel to *Bloodstone*?

A year ago I would have said no. A lot of things that happen in the book don't seem to lend themselves very well to a sequel. But an idea did come to mind fairly recently, and I think it's a pretty good one. Leisure's releasing *The Reach* as my next novel, which is a very different type of read than *Bloodstone*, leaner and closer to a thriller, and I've just turned in a third novel that's more straight horror. I've started writing another new one, but I might just dive into a *Bloodstone* sequel after that if people seem to want it, and if I get inspired by the story.

I'd like to say thanks to everyone who has supported me and my career. I'm amazed and humbled by the reaction I've received so far. The first draft of *Bloodstone* was written nearly ten years ago now, and I've changed a lot as a writer and a person since then. But I'm happy that the novel has seemed to touch a lot of people, and that so many are willing to take a chance on a relatively new writer. I'm very curious to see how people react to *The Reach*. Anyone who'd like to get in touch can reach me through my website. I'm always happy to talk to readers!

Books by Nate Kenyon

Bloodstone (2005) Hardcover Five Star Books
    (2008) Mass-market paperback Leisure Books
The Reach (2008) Mass-market paperback Leisure Books
The Bone Factory (2009) Mass-market paperback Leisure Books
Prime (2009) Trade paperback Apex Books
Sparrow Rock (2010) Mass-market paperback Leisure Books

Awards

P&E Horror Novel of the Year for *Bloodstone*

> "There's a whole spectrum of pain awaiting us out here in the world all the time — physical and emotional. If you decide you're going to essay the subject of pain — and you do it well — you make the reader feel it, identify with it, just like any other experience or emotion."
>
> — *Jack Ketchum*

Old Flames: Jack Ketchum
by Amy Grech and Michael McCarty

"*Who's the scariest guy in America? Probably Jack Ketchum*"— Stephen King.

He is named after a train robber (Black Jack Ketchum), praised by such giants of the genre as Stephen King, Robert Bloch, Bentley Little, Edward Lee, Richard Laymon and Ed Gorman. Jack Ketchum writes high-voltage horror. You don't get novels this electrifying unless you bite into a toaster with your braces.

Shocking? Yes.

Scary? You betcha.

Sick? Yes, he is one sick puppy.

Jack Ketchum is the pseudonym for a former actor, singer, teacher, literary agent, lumber salesman, and soda jerk — a former flower child and baby boomer who figures that in 1956, Elvis, dinosaurs and horror probably saved his life.

His first novel, Off Season, prompted The Village Voice *to publicly scold its publisher in print for publishing violent pornography. He personally disagrees but is perfectly happy to let you decide for yourself. His short story "The Box" won a 1994 Bram Stoker Award from the Horror Writers Association and his story* Gone *won in 2000 — and in 2003 he won Stokers for both best collection for* Peaceable Kingdom *and best long fiction for* Closing Time. *He has written 11 novels, the latest of which are* Red, Ladies' Night, *and* The Lost. *His stories are also collected in* The Exit at Toledo Blade Boulevard *and* Broken on the Wheel of Sex.

His novella Old Flames *is available as a limited edition hardcover from Cemetery Dance and as a mass-market paperback from Leisure Horror. Stephen King cited Jack's novella* The Crossings *in his speech at the 2003 National Book Awards.*

Bloodletting Press published Book of Souls, *a collection of nonfiction memoirs by Jack. Collected in this volume are* Henry Miller *and* the Push *(originally published in* Exit at Toledo Blade Boulevard*),* The Dust of the Heavens *(originally published as a chapbook from James Cahill),* Risky Living: A Memoir *(originally published as an afterward to the Gauntlet Press edition of* Hide and Seek*), and* Us Again *(Jack's reminiscences of 9/11).*

When is extreme horror too extreme for Jack Ketchum?

When there's no point to it. Graphic for graphic's sake. When it's predictable.

Your books *Red*, *The Girl Next Door* and *The Lost* all have been turned into movies. Of the three, which one do you feel is truest to the book and why?

I think I've been amazingly lucky in that all three have been quite true to the source material. Each of them have diverted here and there, of course — the brief love affair was cut from *Red*, the coda eliminated from *The Lost*, Ruth's death scene changed in *The Girl Next Door* — but they're movies, so you expect changes. But the *feel* of each of the books is there, the emotional weight is true. And damned if I'm picking one.

Dallas Mayr, better known to the world as Jack Ketchum (photograph by Claudio Sforza, 2007).

You and Clive Barker are famous for writing about the different levels of pain. Pain is an individual experience; how do you give it mass-market appeal?

There's a whole spectrum of pain awaiting us out here in the world all the time — physical and emotional. If you decide you're going to essay the subject of pain — and you do it well — you make the reader feel it, identify with it, just like any other experience or emotion. And identifying with a character or characters is probably the main reason fiction is appealing in the first place. You don't usually read a novel through to the end because you find the setting appealing. It's the characters and the situations they find themselves in that capture you.

Your relentless novel *The Girl Next Door* challenges the reader to consider what they know about pain as they witness an unthinkable act. What inspired you to write this book?
The true story behind it — the murder of Sylvia Likens. There are exceptions, like *The Executioner's Song* and *In Cold Blood,* but often fiction can do what just telling the facts of a story can't do. So I'd considered a true-crime approach and discarded the idea because I thought that I could — through characters, through what they see and feel and do — bring the story home to readers on a far more personal level. Really hurt you with it. The strength of fiction is that it frees the imagination by its very nature. People with little imagination usually don't read novels. Those that do, can be reached almost as though they were experiencing these things themselves.

When Stephen King wrote *The Dead Zone,* his antagonist killed a dog and he received several angry letters from pet lovers. In the beginning of *Red,* the protagonist's dog is killed. Did you receive several angry letters too? Are you a pet owner?
I grew up with dogs but since college, when I took up apartment living, it's been cats. Now I can't imagine life without them. I have four of them — Zoey, Cujo, George and Gracie. I never got angry letters from *anybody*, really — reviewers excepted — until the movie *The Girl Next Door* got widely distributed and a movie tie-in edition of the book was published. Since then I've even had a couple of death threats. I wrote to Steve King and said, "Look! I've joined your club!"

You write both extreme horror and kids' books and do it well. Is it harder or easier to write for kids?
I've only written one book for kids, called *The Sandcastle,* and it's never been published. Anyone out there interested? You must be referring to *The Transformed Mouse,* which started out its life as a kids' book and which I turned into a fable for adults. I don't find it any easier or harder. It's fiction. You find the characters, tone, and story and you run with it.

Which do you find more difficult to write: novels or short stories?
Novels. Largely because they're more difficult to start. With a novel, you're talking about a marriage. With a story, it's a brief affair. Contemplating marriage, at least for me, is a lot more daunting.

When you start a new project, be it a collaboration, a novel or short story, do you work from an outline or notes, or do you run with the story wherever your characters take you?

I hate outlines. They kill the fun, the spontaneity. I have a three-quarter wrap-around bulletin board and I work from that. As far as I'm concerned, whoever invented post-a-note stick-um pads deserves the Nobel Prize for Literature.

Why do you write most of your work set in New England? Do you think New England is scarier than elsewhere in America?

Most of my stuff, though by no means all, seems to call for characters in relative isolation. There's still plenty of that in New England. I've found it in New Jersey, though, in Greece, along the Mexican border — even in Florida.

What's next for you?

I've written two movies this year, an adaptation of my novel *Offspring*, which ModernCine have already shot and which is now in post-production — they did *The Girl Next Door*. That should be out early next year. Also an adaptation of my novella *Old Flames*, which has been optioned by Chris Sivertson, the director of *The Lost*. Next summer Leisure will publish *Cover*, which last saw paperback in a barely distributed Warner edition way back in 1987. There are a couple of new short stories in the offing, and *Broken of the Wheel of Sex*. Next for me at the writing desk is probably a short half-hour film, about which I can't say much at the moment.

Writers are advised to "take chances" in their writing. What does taking chances mean to Jack Ketchum?

Write what you like to write, when you want to write it, not what you think might sell big time. If it does, fine. If not, no problem. Have fun.

What advice would you give to a writer after they published their first novel?

Don't be afraid of writing the second one. Don't get worried that you're a one-hit wonder. That can really mess with your brain — I know it did for me. Chances are that if you gave birth to one decent novel, your hips are wide enough to give birth to another.

Last words?

You mean like an epitaph? I like the real Jack Ketchum's last words on the gallows. "I'll be in hell before you finish breakfast, boys! Let 'er rip!"

Books by Jack Ketchum

Off Season (1980)
Hide and Seek (1984)
Cover (1987)
The Girl Next Door (1989)
She Wakes (1989)
Offspring (1991)
Joyride (1994) (aka *Road Kill*)
Strangehold (1995) (aka *Only Child*)
Red (1995)
Ladies Night (1997)
The Exit at Toledo Blade Boulevard (1998)
Right to Life and 2 Stories (1998)
The Dust of the Heavens (1998)
Broken on the Wheel of Sex (1999)
Father and Son (1999)
Masks (1999)
Cover (2000)
Ephemera (2000)
The Lost (2001)
Station Two (2001)
Honor System (2002)
Peaceable Kingdom (2002)
Right to Life (2002)
At Home with the VCR
Sleep Disorder (2003)
The Crossings (2004)
Seascape (2005)
Absinthe (2006)
Weed Species (2006)
Closing Time and Other Stories (2007)
Book of Souls (2008)
Old Flames (2008)
Triage (2008)

Film Adaptations

The Lost (2005)
The Girl Next Door (2007)
Red (2008)

Awards

Bram Stoker Winner for Short Story 1994, "The Box"
Bram Stoker Winner for Short Story 2000, "Gone"
Bram Stoker Winner for Long Fiction 2003, "Closing"
Bram Stoker Winner for Collection 2003, *Peaceable Kingdom*

"Karen only writes when she has to. She's not driven."
—Joe Lansdale

"Joe always says he's passionate, but not obsessed. Obsession takes away a lot of life. Passion drives the writing, but it leaves room for life."
—Karen Lansdale

Till Death Do Us Part: Joe R. and Karen Lansdale

He is known for writing such cult classics as Bubba-Ho Tep, Zeppelins West *and* The Drive-In.

She is known as a writer and editor. She has co-edited Dark at Heart *with her husband and co-edited a story in* Till Death Do Us Part. *She has even penned the short story "Screw Up" with her hubby, And if that isn't enough, she is Joe's business manager too.*

They live in Nacogdoches, Texas, and are known as "Mr. and Mrs. Lansdale" or "Joe and Karen" to their friends. No strangers to the HWA [Horror Writers Association], they have been in the organization since the early days.

How did you two first meet and how long have you been married?

KL: We met in an anthropology class in 1973 at Stephen F. Austin State University in Nacogdoches, Texas. Joe was majoring in anthropology at the time, though he changed the major to humanities and never graduated. I graduated with a double major, Sociology/Criminology. For Joe it was love at first sight. I thought about it awhile. But not a long while.

What is the secret of a happy marriage?

JL & KL: We never really thought about it. It just is. I'm sure there are reasons, but it really has a lot to do with two people who just clicked. We fill in each other's weaknesses. We stay true to who we are, and yet, we have created a separate entity that is us. And we love us just fine.

Karen Lansdale and Joe Lansdale at Lansdale's Self Defense Systems, Shen Chuan, Martial Science Is the school and system (photograph by Adam Coats, 2010).

You are both writers. How do you get along without driving each other crazy? Do you have separate offices?
    JL: Oh heavens no. Karen only writes when she has to. She's not driven.
    KL: Joe always says he's passionate, but not obsessed. Obsession takes away a lot of life. Passion drives the writing, but it leaves room for life. But a large part of his life is writing. And martial arts. But mostly family. We have computers side by side and we share the same office, because we like it that way.

What was the Horror Writers Association during the early days. What was the beginning of the organization like? What did you contribute to the HWA?
    KL: The beginning was a list of names who were interested in the organization. That's as far as Rick (Robert McMammon) wanted to go. He liked the idea, put an advertisement in a newspaper somewhere about THE HORROR OCCULT WRITERS LEAGUE — HOWL, but when the interest poured in he decided he didn't want to do it. I volunteered and Joe and Rick and others helped. Dean Koontz finally took over and turned it from a photocopied newsletter with smatterings of this and that into a working and professional organization.

I heard that Dean Koontz left the HWA because he felt the organization was too focused on the Bram Stoker Awards. Do you know if that is true? And what are your opinions about that?

JL: Dean would have to speak for himself, but I do know all of us who first put it together, and that would be Karen and Rick and Joe and Dean, thought there shouldn't be awards. Awards are all right, and not a terrible idea, except that they often become the totality of an organization.

If you were to compare yourselves to a famous couple, would it be: Brad Pitt and Angelina Jolie, Brad Pitt and Jennifer Annison, Billy Bob Thornton and Angelina Jolie, Lyle Lovett and Julia Roberts, Julius Caesar and Cleopatra, or Other?

KL: We would compare ourselves to a not so famous couple. Joe and Karen Lansdale.

Have you ever thought of writing a novel together? Have you ever collaborated together? What is the secret of working together and keep a happy marriage?

KL: I keep the books and run the writing and the martial arts business. That's enough writing. I've only written when I had to, and to help Joe finish a story where we were asked to write together as a married couple, and one where he couldn't make the ending work and we needed the money! We edited an anthology together. That could happen again, but don't hold your breath. We also collaborated with our son on a children's book forthcoming titled *In Waders from Mars*. He told the story to his dad when he was four or five, and Joe wrote it down, and I wrote the ending. Joe and I would never write a book together. Maybe that's why we've been happily married for 35 years.

Joe, what can you tell us about "Bubba Nosferatu?"

JL: "Bubba Nosferatu" is Don's (Coscarelli) baby. I'm it's grandparent, but he's doing that. I just recently heard about it. I do expect a check from that deal. I wish him luck. I love Don and think he's a great and original filmmaker.

Any advice for beginning writers?

JL: Once upon a time you wrote a story and put it in an envelope with return postage and sent it to the editor of the magazine where you wanted to appear, and they either returned it or bought it. My favorite was when they'd send a check back directly. Those days are gone. It's harder and harder to sell without an agent. The exception to that is short stories. I love short stories, and though there may not be as many markets as there once were, there are quite a few, especially if you're willing to go to on-line markets as well.

Short stories help you build a reputation and that helps you get an agent.

But remember this, an agent can't sell something you can't sell, they just have more time to mess with it than you do. There job is to make money off of your work, and yours is to write and make money off your work. So agents are a necessary thing these days; long cry from when I managed my own career and sold my own short stories. It wasn't a big living, more like a part time job that didn't pay very well, but it sure helped me hone my craft. Good short stories teach you how to engage the reader and write nice, interesting, tight chapters.

I find that so many writers are so worried about having an agent, that they forget they need to have the craft and the material first. That's the way to start. Write. Publish short stories. An agent most likely won't handle those anyway, as there's no money in it for them. But when you've got enough sales, some credits, and then you want to write that novel, then the agent might be more interested in listening.

DO IT FIRST. Then worry about selling it.

Last words?
KL: Joe's Brother Andrew Vachss says: Stay strong.

"I was surprised Bubba Ho-Tep was chosen, as it struck me as being difficult to film. But I was pleased with the results. I couldn't have fared better for my first time out. Well, unless it were a big hit. This one is going to be seen again and again, and be a cult and collector's film. I'm proud of it."

— *Joe R. Lansdale*

Bubba Ho-Tep: Joe R. Lansdale

Joe R. Lansdale's writing is as spicy as a pot of Texas chili cooked all day on the range.

Texan Lansdale has been writing for over two decades and has over twenty novels, in addition to story collections, anthologies and novellas, to his credit. They include The Drive-In, The Magic Wagon, Razored Saddles, The Two Bear Mambo, Bad Chili, The Night Runners, *and* On the Farside of the Cadillac Desert with Dead Folks. *His latest novel is* A Fine Dark Line.

He has won five Bram Stoker Awards, a British Fantasy Award, the American Mystery Award, the Horror Critics Award and many others. He lives in Nacogdoches, Texas, with his wife Karen, who is a writer and editor.

Lansdale has been a student of the martial arts for more than thirty years. He's a two-time inductee into the International Martial Arts Hall of Fame. He founded Shen Chuan, Martial Science.

His novella Bubba Ho-Tep *was turned into a movie starring Bruce Campbell of* Evil Dead *fame, Ossie Davis and Reggie Bannister from the* Phantasm *series.*

Is there much of a difference between Northern and Southern writers?

I think there is, though perhaps not as great a difference as there once was. The South seems preoccupied with off-the-wall characters, a kind of gothic atmosphere. I think it makes Southern writing interesting. Texas writing is similar to Southern writing, but it has a flavor all its own. Several. It's a big state and all the parts are different. Where I live is more Southern.

Texas is so wrapped up in myth and legend, it's hard to know what the state and its people are really about. Real Texans, raised on these myths and legends, sometimes become legends themselves. The bottom line is, Texas and its people are pretty much what most people mean when they use the broader term "America." No state represents the independent spirit, the can-do attitude of America, better than Texas.

Were you surprised that Don A. Coscarelli, the director and writer of the *Phantasm* movies, turned your novella *Bubba Ho-Tep* into a movie?

I was surprised *Bubba* was chosen, as it struck me as being difficult to film. But I was pleased with the results. I couldn't have fared better for my first time out. Well, unless it were a big hit. This one is going to be seen again and again, and be a cult and collector's film. I'm proud of it.

You have been writing since the '80s. How did you survive the '90s, when the suits said horror was dead?

Horror may well have been dead. I started out writing crime and moved into horror, as I liked them both, but by the '90s I wasn't writing much in the way of horror. I was accepted as a crime writer, but it wasn't entirely planned. I just went back to doing what I started out to do and the timing was good. I think I've survived by moving around and doing what I like, which goes against standard advice.

How many publishers saw *The Magic Wagon* before it was published by Doubleday?

Only one publisher saw it, Doubleday. I sold it verbally to Pat LoBrutto, who then asked for a general outline, maybe a chapter or two, I don't remember.

The Magic Wagon **has some wonderful,** colorful characters such as Rot Toe the Wrestling Chimpanzee, Buster Foggs and Old Albert. Are any of them based on real people?

Joe Lansdale in the backyard of his Texas home (photographed by Karen Lansdale, 1997).

In this book they aren't based on anyone, though there were wrestling chimpanzees that went with fairs, and wrestled volunteers for money. I saw something about that on TV and went with it.

You have written *The Drive-In* and *The Drive-In 2*. If you had a real drive-in theater, what movies would you show?

Oh, the movies in the book, and plenty of others. I'm not as nuts about the old bad ones as I once was. But there are certainly the usual suspects that are actually good films—*Phantasm, Texas Chain Saw Massacre, Night of the Living Dead* and *Bubba Ho-Tep*—and it has to do with them being great and having a wonderful atmosphere, not because I think they're low-budget films. They each are special in their own way.

What would you like to say about your latest books *A Fine Dark Line* and *For a Few Stories More*?

For a Few Stories More was done for the fans, a companion piece to *The Good, the Bad and the Indifferent*. It wasn't done for the mass market. The introductions are more interesting than most of the stories, but they show the growth of a writer and are for those who are interested in that. *A Fine Dark Line* is my new one. Subterranean did the uncut version, which is not my preferred version, but is interesting because it's close to what came out of the machine, with some cuts, many of which are in the back. I mentioned certain things I'd cut and that they were in the back to read, and some of them weren't. I messed up there. But it's a special edition with introductions and some unique material.

Of your collective works, what are your favorite short stories and novels?

"Night They Missed the Horror Show," "Stepping Out, Summer 68," and "Mr. Weedeater." Today. Tomorrow I may like others. Novels: *The Bottoms, Mucho Mojo, The Drive-In*, though tomorrow I may like others. I really like the collection *High Cotton*, and it's my best short stuff. Of novellas, *On the Far Side of the Cadillac Desert with Dead Folks, Bubba Ho-Tep*, which I wasn't nuts about at the time of the writing, and *The Big Blow*, both the novella and the short novel version.

You have written some movie scripts. Have any of them been on the silver screen or video screens?

I've sold a couple of scripts, but neither got produced, and another has been optioned several times. I was also hired to revise a script for a French director, but he didn't like it. *Dead in the West* gets optioned repeatedly.

You are friends with Dean Koontz. Care to share an anecdote about the Master of Suspense?

Dean once called me and described a bug that was in his kitchen and he wanted me to identify it. He doesn't like bugs and wanted it dead. Which was done, I think, by an exterminator. It's been a while, but that's how I remember it.

Besides the horror and crime novels, you have written some Batman material, including "Terror on the High Skies" and "Captured by the Engines" for the animated *Batman* series and a couple of Batman short stories. Were you attracted to the character because he's a dark superhero?

I grew up on Batman, and actually, in the '50s, he was a two-fisted, honest, try-not-to-kill-the-bad-guy hero. But there was always some sort of implied darkness there, especially in *Detective Comics*. I like a hero who is at heart a Boy Scout, but has had to adjust that thinking to the real world. My favorite Batman work I've done is the *Batman* animated series, "Read My Lips," "Showdown" and maybe my all-time favorite, "Perchance to Dream." "Critters" was fun, but the series had changes by then, dumbed down a bit and designed to appeal primarily to kids, where before it did that and appealed to adults as well.

I loved doing "Captured by the Engines" because I played Batman as real as possible within the context of a superhero universe, and even did a bit of writing experimentation. Of the two short stories, "Subway Jack" is a favorite because it's a perfect pulp piece with a kind of literary sensibility, and I got to use experimental approaches, comic frames, film, audio, the whole nine yards.

"Terror on the High Skies" was done for young kids, so I used the Batman of the '50s for that, the one I grew up on, with the weird gadgets, strange villain plans (a pirate ship that floats in the air), etc. It was a lot of fun and struck me as an episode of the comic from that era, though through the eyes of a kid.

Books by Joe R. Lansdale

HAP COLLINS AND LEONARD PINE MYSTERIES

Savage Season (1990)
Mucho Mojo (Cemetery Dance Publications, 1994)
Two-Bear Mambo (1995)
Bad Chili (1997)
Rumble Tumble (1998)
Veil's Visit (includes the eponymous story, written with Andrew Vachss) (1999) (limited edition)

Captains Outrageous (2001)
Vanilla Ride (2009)

THE "DRIVE-IN" SERIES

The Drive-In: A "B" Movie with Blood and Popcorn, Made in Texas (1988)
The Drive-In 2: Not Just One of Them Sequels (1989)
The Drive-In: A Double-Feature (1997, omnibus) compiles the first two
The Drive-In: The Bus Tour (2005) (limited edition)

THE "NED THE SEAL" TRILOGY

These are all limited editions published by Subterranean Press
Zeppelins West (2001)
Flaming London (2006)

OTHER NOVELS

Act of Love (1980)
Texas Night Riders (1983) (originally published under the pseudonym Ray Slater)
Dead in the West (1986) (written in 1980)
Magic Wagon (1986)
The Nightrunners (1987) (written in 1982 as *Night of the Goblins*)
Cold in July (1989)
Tarzan: the Lost Adventure (1995) (with Edgar Rice Burroughs)
The Boar (1998) (initially a limited edition, later republished)
Freezer Burn (1999)
Waltz of Shadows (1999) (written in 1991) (limited edition "Lost Lansdale" vol. 1)
Something Lumber This Way Comes (1999) (Children's book) (limited. "Lost Lansdale" vol. 2)
The Big Blow (2000) (limited edition)
Blood Dance (2000) (written in the early '80's) (limited edition "Lost Lansdale" vol. 3)
The Bottoms (2000)
A Fine Dark Line (2002)
Sunset and Sawdust (2004)
Lost Echoes (2007)
Leather Maiden (2008)

PSEUDONYMOUS NOVELS

Molly's Sexual Follies (as Brad Simmons) Pseudonymous porn novel written with Brad Foster

MARK STONE: MIA HUNTER SERIES

These are a few novels Lansdale wrote under the pseudonym "Jack Buchanan." They were probably co-written with Stephen Mertz. Some people erroneously report that Lansdale is responsible for the entire series, which is definitely not true.

Hanoi Deathgrip (Stone: MIA Hunter #3)
Mountain Massacre (Stone: MIA Hunter #4)
Saigon Slaughter (the consensus seems to be that this is #7, though some claim #8)

SHORT STORIES COLLECTIONS

By Bizarre Hands (1989)
Stories by Mama Lansdale's Youngest Boy (1991) aka Author's Choice Monthly #18
Bestsellers Guaranteed (1993)
Electric Gumbo: A Lansdale Reader (1994) (Quality Paperback Book Club exclusive)
Writer of the Purple Rage (1994)
A Fistfull of Stories (and Articles) (1996)
The Good, the Bad, and the Indifferent (1997) (limited edition)
Private Eye Action, as You Like It (1998) (with Lewis Shiner) (limited edition)
Triple Feature (1999) (limited edition)
The Long Ones: Nuthin' but Novellas (2000)
High Cotton (2000)
For a Few Stories More (2002) (limited edition "Lost Lansdale" vol. 4; the "ultra-limited" edition of this book included a previously unpublished Young Adult vampire novel called *Shadow Time*, which has not appeared anywhere else)
A Little Green Book of Monster Stories (2003) (limited edition)
Bumper Crop (2004)
Mad Dog Summer and Other Stories (2004) (initially a limited edition, reissued in paperback)
The King: and Other Stories (2005) (limited edition)
God of the Razor and Other Stories (2007)
The Shadows, Kith and Kin (2007)
Sanctified and Chicken-Fried: The Portable Lansdale (2009)

CHAPBOOKS

On the Far Side of the Cadillac Desert With Dead Folks (1991) (limited edition)
The Steel Valentine (1991) (Pulphouse Hardback Magazine #7)
Steppin' Out, Summer '68 (1992) (limited edition)
God of the Razor (1992) (limited edition)
Tight Little Stitches In A Dead Man's Back (1992) (limited edition)
My Dead Dog Bobby (1995) (limited edition)
Bubba Ho-Tep (2003) (novella) (published standalone as a movie tie-in)
Duck Footed (2005) (novella) (limited edition)

Awards

He's won numerous awards in the genre including sixteen Bram Stoker Awards, the Grand Master Award from the World Horror Convention, a British Fantasy Award, the American Mystery Award, the Horror Critics Award, the Grinzane Cavour Prize for Literature, the "Shot in the Dark" International Crime Writer's Award, the Golden Lion Award, the Booklist Editor's Award, the Critic's Choice Award, and a New York Times Notable Book Award.

"After I abandoned doing *My Work Is Not Yet Done* as a screenplay, my plan was to write it as a novel of 300 pages or so. But that would entail far too much material that is extraneous to the core of the narrative. In its present form, *My Work Is Not Yet Done* is a short novel, which is a separate genre from a novella."

—*Thomas Ligotti*

Puppets, Nightmares and Gothic Splendor: Thomas Ligotti
by Mark McLaughlin and Michael McCarty

If you were to ask most aficionados of fright fiction to name the most sophisticated and literate of today's horror writers, chances are that one name would be on all of their lips: Thomas Ligotti. Many believe he is the heir to the thrones of both Edgar Allan Poe and H.P. Lovecraft, and some will insist he's better than either one. People who enjoy the works of Ligotti have very strong opinions about his work.

Like Poe and Lovecraft, Ligotti is primarily known for his short fiction. His story collections—from *Songs of a Dead Dreamer* to *Grimscribe: His Lives and Works* to *The Nightmare Factory* and more—are noted for their nightmarish Gothic surrealism. Even though the majority of his stories take place in the present day, they have a timeless quality to them. They could be set in the 1800s or even 500 years from now. In Ligotti's twilight dreamworlds, the past, present and future all blur together, and nothing is as it seems.

You worked in Detroit for over two decades. Did seeing those all those abandoned, decayed buildings influence your dark, brooding fiction?

I would say they inspired me more than influenced me. I've never been one for realism, so what I rendered in a number of my stories was the impressionistic effect on me of Detroit's desolation rather than its details. In "The Chymist" I mention several locales that I fabricated but which have their counterparts in Detroit. Same thing with "The Red Tower" and "The Bungalow House." And I mentally set the whole of *My Work Is Not Yet Done* in Detroit, although I never name the city. There's a book called *American Ruins* by Camilo José Vergara that features a number of Detroit's most desolate spots. Vergara proposed to the Detroit City Council that a section of the city's downtown area be set aside as an "urban ruins theme park." They thought he was crazy, of course, and dismissed the idea.

Whoever wants to get a sense of what a run-down marvel Detroit has become should rent the movie *Narc*, which is set entirely in Detroit. And at the end of *Transformers*, when all the robots have their battle royal, much of that is set in Detroit. I didn't know this before I saw the movie, but I immediately recognized the downtown district where these scenes were shot. Later I verified that they were indeed filmed in an area of Detroit where I worked for over twenty years.

From your fiction, one might imagine that you grew up in gloomy Gothic surroundings, like the House of Usher. How close is that fanciful notion to reality?

I lived in Detroit for the first couple years of my life, and I visited my grandparents there quite often during my childhood. They lived in a bungalow. I also spent a lot of time in the '60s hanging out in a dope house district of Detroit's east side. For the most part, though, I was raised in an upper-class suburb of Detroit called Grosse Pointe. My family didn't live in one of those grand old piles down by Lakeshore Drive, but I had friends who did. It's a shame that every one of the original Victorian mansions in Grosse Pointe was torn down before I was born, but their replacements were still architecturally daunting.

Tell us about your inspirations for your short story collection *Grimscribe*.

There was no single inspiration for the stories in that collection. The publisher wanted to try and pass off a collection of stories as a sort of novel, so I went along with this really embarrassingly transparent ruse. It would be too boring for the majority of the readers of this interview to go through the stories one by one.

The stories in that book are all fascinating and far from boring, but you're right — at first glance, it does look like a novel. Recently, the story "The Frolic" from your collection *Songs of a Dead Dreamer* was made into a short film.

My script collaborator Brandon Trenz and I knew a producer named Jane Kosek. She used to work with us at a publishing company in Detroit. Then she lit out for Hollywood. She and Brandon went to see an agent in LA about shopping some of our scripts around, but that led nowhere. She'd worked with a number of directors and suggested to one of them doing "The Frolic" as a short film. That didn't work at all because the director had all these loopy ideas for the film. Some years later, she showed the story to another director, Jacob Cooney, and he was amenable to doing something that was closer to what Brandon and I had in mind for the film version.

Have any of your other works been optioned for movies?
All of the stories in *The Nightmare Factory* are part of an exclusive option-to-buy agreement with Fox Atomic. So they can do pretty anything they want with them until the option runs out. That's how the comic book versions of some of my stories came about. I think that *My Work Is Not Yet Done* is the most viable thing I've written for the purposes of a movie adaptation. Actually, the story was originally conceived as a film script. A paperback version of the book came out in June 2010 from Virgin Books.

The Nightmare Factory has a crumbling asylum in it. Was that based on a real facility?
No. The title of that book was just something I came up with. Later I discovered that same title had been used for a poetry collection by Maxine Kumin.

The Agonizing Resurrection of Victor Frankenstein and Other Gothic Tales is a very hard book to find these days. What inspired you to write about the world's most famous mad scientist?
A woman named Tina Said was doing a fanzine that used only short prose. She asked me to contribute something and I wrote "One Thousand Painful Variations Performed Upon Divers Creatures Undergoing the Treatment of Dr. Moreau, Humanist." Then I wrote two more pieces for a fanzine called *Grimoire* that the prose poet Thomas Wiloch, another friend of mine from work, was doing, and that we ended up putting out together. After that, I just kept writing miniature variations on famous horror stories and films until I got tired of doing them. I tried to take the variations into even more tragic and nightmarish territory than the originals. One critic described the pieces in *Agonizing Resurrection* as an "apotheosis of torment." That's what I was going for — the absolute worst doom that I could imagine for the main characters in these stories — although most readers thought they were just *jeux d'esprits*. Some of them were published by Harry Morris in his Silver Scarab Press edition of my first collection, *Songs of a Dead Dreamer*.

What was the first horror movie you ever saw?
Tarantula.

How often do you watch horror movies? What was the last one you watched?
I rent horror movies whenever I think they might be good, or at least watchable. The last one I rented was *The Ruins*. The author of the book on which the movie was based did the screenplay, so I thought there was a chance it would be okay, since he also adapted his previous book, *A Simple Plan*, into a terrific movie. There was a lot of "intense gore" in *The Ruins*, but I don't respond to that sort of thing no matter how intense it is. They're only movies, after all. I don't think I would have rented *The Ruins* at all if I didn't get it out of one of the "movie cubes" at the local supermarket for a buck. On the whole, I'm not a fan of horror movies. I'd rather watch political thrillers, courtroom dramas, caper films, plain old suspense, and the like.

What was the inspiration for *My Work Is Not Yet Done*? And do you see a lot of yourself in the protagonist Frank Domino?
The character's surname is actually Dominio. It's only his boss who mockingly mutilates his name into Domino. I used this moniker because in one of its meanings is a domino, a kind of hooded costume that resembles the figure of death. At the time I wrote *My Work Is Not Yet Done* I was having some troubles at work very similar to those of the protagonist. Naturally, these situations, which are very common in workplaces, inspire certain fantasies. Rather than just fantasizing, I wrote a story in which I took those fantasies several steps further than anyone could in real life. None of the characters in *My Work Is Not Yet Done* is based on the persons I was having trouble with. But I did think of Frank Dominio as a psycho killer version of myself, although he didn't start out that way. The whole experience taught me that forgetting is the best revenge. I also concluded that murder is a really lame form of vengeance. Non-existence is just too good for some people.

My Work Is Not Yet Done and your story "The Shadow at the Bottom of the World" are thematically similar. Do you see them as companion pieces?
I really don't see the resemblance myself. "The Shadow at the Bottom of the World" is a horror hymn to autumn, or that's the way I thought of it. "Shadow" is one of those stories in which the people of a small town share the same barbaric impulse, although the reason for this impulse is left a mystery. It would have undermined the point of the story to give the reason for this bloodthirsty impulse. There is no reason I could have given anyway because it's wholly irrational. Blood sacrifice in certain ancient cultures seemingly had a profit motive in appeasing gods or whatever.

But it's quite apparent that people of all times have been drawn to murder in any form, real or fictional. This is no great psychological or sociological observation. It's only a fact. We are lovers of havoc and evil. A tranquil existence is intolerable to us. Think of the famous cuckoo clock soliloquy spoken by the character Harry Lime in the movie *The Third Man*. The rest of the world holds in contempt any country that is not populated by ambitious bloodletters. Think of all the jokes about Canadians or Scandinavians. Of course, the citizens of these lands once had their day. I suppose that since *My Work Is Not Yet Done* exults in supernatural mayhem, it's another example of this impulse. But this impulse is also explored as a force beyond our control in the form of a Schopenhauerian Will that is at the source of what we are when we're not playing at being "civilized." Frank Dominio gradually comes to realize this in the course of the narrative.

My Work Is Not Yet Done is 42,000 words, the closest you've come so far to writing a novel. Have you ever thought about expanding it into a novel?

After I abandoned doing *My Work Is Not Yet Done* as a screenplay, my plan was to write it as a novel of 300 pages or so. But that would entail far too much material that is extraneous to the core of the narrative. In its present form, *My Work Is Not Yet Done* is a short novel, which is a separate genre from a novella. It has the structure of a novel, but not what most people would consider the length. Plenty of books that readers think of as novels are really short novels. Albert Camus' *The Stranger*, James M. Cain's *The Postman Always Rings Twice*, Truman Capote's *Breakfast at Tiffany's*, Robert Louis Stevenson's *The Strange Case of Dr. Jekyll and Mr. Hyde*, Ray Bradbury's *Fahrenheit 451*, Thomas Pychon's *The Crying of Lot 49*, J.D. Salinger's *Catcher in the Rye*, Voltaire's *Candide*, Lovecraft's novels, William Hope Hodgson's *The House on the Borderland*, and the list goes on. The short story is still the best form for horror fiction, but the short novel isn't bad either. It keeps horror writers from letting the kernel of their narratives wander too far out of sight. The American poet and short novelist Howard Nemerov wrote an interesting study of the short novel in a collection of his critical essays. I mean, I don't care if *My Work Is Not Yet Done* is called a novella, a short novel, or roach trap. But there is such a thing as a short novel.

Your work has been compared many times to that of H.P. Lovecraft. How do you feel about the comparison? If Lovecraft were still alive, do you think you two would get along?

I think the comparison with Lovecraft is always meant to be a compliment to me. I would say there is a likeness between Lovecraft and me in that our narratives are focused on a supernatural or weird element and nothing else. Lovecraft said as much of his own stories, and I feel intuitively that he was right. As for getting along with Lovecraft, it wasn't too long ago that I had a conversation with Jason Van Hollander about this. Both of us agreed that we would probably find Lovecraft a difficult person to be around because his gentlemanly behavior would get on our nerves. Of course, I can't be sure of that because Lovecraft had such a great sense of humor, and my own views are compatible with his on just about every subject. But if Lovecraft visited me, I think I would have to watch my words and not say anything like, "Fuck me, I ran out of cigarettes." It's not that I think Lovecraft was prudish. From reading his letters, one can tell that he wasn't shockable. He just had firm ideas about how people should present themselves, and that didn't include using profane language or tobacco, two things I find impossible not to do. I can't fault him for that.

Dreams play an important role in many of your stories. What do you dream about?

It's been my experience that mostly I dream about what I've seen and what I've done. So I have a lot of dreams about things like not being able to find my car in a parking garage. But I also have the kind of strange dreams that everyone has. The first "dream monologue" in "The Bungalow House" where the protagonist feels a sense of ecstatic terror while standing in the dim and rank living room of the eponymous structure and sensing all those insects around him was based on a dream I had. I also dreamed about those weird locales in "Gas Station Carnivals." And the literally feculent building in "The Night School." Perhaps the most affecting dream I've ever had was the one that led to my writing "The Cocoons." I'd had recurrent dreams for some time about humans being transformed into some bizarre life form that served as food for other bizarre life forms. When I woke up from that dream, I felt I had gone mad and would remain that way.

I have to say that I find dreaming to be among the most wretched experiences forced on human beings. It denies you the relief of sleep, which is supposed to knit up the raveled sleeve of care. But if you always wake up with a dream in your head, it feels like you've been dreaming all night, and that you've never gotten any respite from conscious existence. Every time I go to bed, I think, "What kind of inane or traumatizing trash am I going to get into tonight?" But if I thought too much about dreaming, I'd never get to sleep. To top it off, I have night terrors in which I'm awake but am paralyzed and feel as if I'm having a heart attack. The only way I can wake up is by screaming, which takes a lot of effort. And then there are those dreams in which I find myself in a place that's supercharged by the presence of something evil that never makes an appearance. How can anyone tell someone to have "Sweet Dreams"? I know that there are dreams that are pleasant and that one regrets awaking from. And that is regret indeed.

Puppets and dolls also figure into your fiction with some frequency. Do you find them frightening?

I did when I was a child, but not since. However, I still find puppets to be uncanny things. For me, the puppet emblemizes the entrapment and manipulation of human beings by forces beyond our control. Obviously, there are a lot of things that people are aware they cannot control in their lives. As *Fireside Theater* brilliantly said, "Your brain is not the boss." In my world, this is an everyday experience because I've been long besieged by abnormal psychological states that cause me to be constantly aware that I have no control over who I am and how I'll act. Most people don't feel this way or they don't notice the controlling forces because they're very subtle. Having any kind of control over your actions or feelings is everybody's illusion. No one can make themselves what they are. It's a totally absurd notion, because if you could make yourself what you are, you'd first have to be a certain way and be able to choose what that way would be. But then you'd also have to be able to choose to choose what way you would be, and on into infinity. There are always determining powers, and those make us the way we are whether or not we realize it. I realize that there are philosophers who have reconciled determinism with free will on paper, and that everyone feels as if they're in control of themselves and take responsibility for their actions. But how many of us can say that we're always, or even often, in control of our thoughts? And if you're not in control of your thoughts, then what are you in control of?

If you doubt this, just see if you can attain an empty mind in the course of meditating. It can be done, I know, because I did it for about 30 years. But it's not easy, and I never found it to do anything more than effect a state of temporary relaxation. And many people can't do it at all because they can't control their thoughts. If anyone out there has achieved a significant alteration in their consciousness due to meditation, I'd love to hear about it. Initially I practiced Transcendental Medication. You have a mantra that you run through your head to keep thoughts from interfering with your meditation. The mantra is supposed to be a secret word that only you know. Then one day some Hari Krishna guy came up to me on the street and told me my mantra. He used to teach Transcendental Meditation and said that it was all a hoax. Then he tried to convert me to his form of hoax. But I kept meditating using what were more traditional and supposedly more effective methods.

Do angels or demons exist?

Not in my experience. But I can imagine someone becoming involved in spiritualism of one kind or another to the extent that he or she would start to believe in all kinds of supernatural things and experience their presence. I once took a series of classes in reading other people's minds, and sure enough

I was able to read other people's minds. It's hard not to give in to the influences that are brought to bear in an environment like that. The only thing you can do to break free is to remove yourself from that environment, or have someone else remove you from it. As Blaise Pascal said, "Men are so necessarily mad that not to be mad would amount to another form of madness." I've tried as hard as I can to become sane, but I've never gotten there.

Which of your books do you consider your best?

My latest collection *Teatro Grottesco*, no doubt. I realize that writers often think that the manuscript in the bottom drawer of their desk is their best work. It's a form of self-hypnosis.

Are you a techno-savvy person? Do you "do" cell phones, iPods, Blackberries?

I have no use for any of those devices, but if I did I would use them. I can't imagine living without a computer with a high-speed modem. There is so much great stuff out there to keep one from thinking about suffering and death.

What's on the horizon for you?

The Conspiracy Against the Human Race: A Short Life of Horror. In this book I tried to bind together themes from pessimistic philosophy and the horror genre into an exposition on the uncanny nature and ontological fraudulence of the human species. The springboard for these themes is a 1933 essay titled "The Last Messiah" by the Norwegian philosopher Peter Wessel Zapffe, who made much of the conspicuous fact that we don't really like to think about the bad things in life and so we repress them in various ways. For instance, by entertaining distractions and working toward a better future, an undertaking that is futile since there will always be a differential between what we have and what we want. Thus, we will be forever discontented with our lives, especially since they all end in some unpleasantness that we're very good at ignoring because if we weren't good at ignoring that unpleasantness our lives would be a nightmare.

A recent writer who has argued that the human race would be better off if it didn't exist is the South African philosopher of ethics David Benatar, whose book *Better Never to Have Been: The Harm of Coming into Existence* cogently lays out why nonexistence is preferable to existence. His argument is that there is an asymmetry between non-painful experience and painful experience which tips the scales in favor of nonexistence. For this reason, Benatar argues, it is immoral to produce children who would never know this imbalance, which often is a very severe imbalance, between nonpainful experience and painful experience — not just necessarily extremely painful experience but any painful experience at all, which is sometimes called the Pinprick

Argument. I've exchanged some emails with Benatar because I discuss his book in my *Conspiracy Against the Human Race* and wanted to take the opportunity to see if he thought I had misrepresented his ideas in any way. He told me that I had not violated his position in any of its major claims, although he did mention some fine points of disagreement between us.

The question that has sometimes arisen in the uniformly negative reviews of Benatar's book is why the author doesn't commit suicide. This is not a surprising reaction on the part of what are often called by nonpessimistic philosophers "healthy adults." Other healthy adults insist that producing a work that is negative on life shows its author to be a hypocrite, because the very act of writing is a sign of being activated by a vital impulse. The first point, that pessimistic thinkers should kill themselves in order to live up to their ideas, exhibits such an inadequacy of intellect and imagination that it really doesn't deserve a response. Just because someone has reached the conclusion that the amount of suffering in this world is so egregious that anyone would be better off never having been born doesn't mean he perforce must commit suicide. It only means that he has concluded that anyone would be better off never having been born. Others may disagree on this point as it pleases them, but they must accept that if they believe themselves to have a better case than the pessimist, then they are mistaken.

On the second point — that pessimists are hypocrites because the very act of writing is a sign of being activated by a vital impulse — all that can be said is that everything that anyone does is activated by a vital impulse. This is much the source of the catastrophe of being alive: We are pushed along day by day by vital impulses, even if some of them lead to suicide. Killing oneself is not a walk in the park by any means. It takes as much initiative as killing someone else, one of the most vital acts of all. Most people think that vitality is emblemized by such things as people in their seventies who water ski or nations that build empires. This way of thinking is simply naïve, but it keeps up our morale because we like to think that we'll be water-skiing when we're in our seventies or be citizens of a nation, or just partners in a business concern, that has built an empire.

Identical with religions that ask of their believers more than they could possibly deliver, pessimism is a set of ideals, not a lifestyle. Those who indict a pessimist either of hypocrisy or pathology are only faking their competence to riddle the mystery of why anyone is the way they are. And no one has yet done that. But to many would-be psycho-biographers, their subjects' pessimism has a two-fold inception: (1) life stories of tribulation, even if the pessimistic caste has no sorrows exclusive to it; (2) a diseased psychology, a charge that pessimists could turn against optimists if the *argumentum ad populum* were not the world's favorite fallacy.

The cover to the 2010 book *The Conspiracy Against the Human Race* by Thomas Ligotti.

If you could have dinner and a conversation with any person past, present or future, who would it be?

I'd like to talk to any intelligent person of adult age who was living on the brink of the extinction of the human race. This is assuming that we'll die out from natural causes and not a catastrophic event. (The latter will almost certainly be the case.) This is also assuming that there will be any intelligent persons living on the brink of the extinction of the human race. So I guess I like to talk to the last living intelligent person. What I'd like to know is whether or not anything significant changed from our time to their time. As always, technology doesn't count as change.

Books by Thomas Ligotti

Songs of a Dead Dreamer, introduction by Ramsey Campbell, (1986) revised and expanded edition, (1989)
Grimscribe (1991)
Noctuary (1994)
The Agonizing Resurrection of Victor Frankenstein and Other Gothic Tales (1994)
The Nightmare Factory (includes "The Red Tower") (1996)
I Have a Special Plan for This World (2000)
This Degenerate Little Town (2001)
My Work Is Not Yet Done: Three Tales of Corporate Horror (2002)
Crampton [with Brandon Trenz] (2003)
Death Poems (2004)
The Frolic [with Brandon Trenz] (2006)
Teatro Grottesco (2007)
The Conspiracy against the Human Race: A Contrivance of Horror (2010)

Awards

1982: Small Press Writers and Artists Organization, Best Author of Horror/Weird Fiction: *The Chymist*
1986: Rhysling Award, from Science Fiction Poetry Association (nomination): *One Thousand Painful Variations Performed Upon Divers Creatures Undergoing the Treatment of Dr. Moreau, Humanist*
1991: World Fantasy Award for Best Short Fiction (nomination): *The Last Feast of Harlequin*
1992: World Fantasy Award for Best Collection (nomination): *Grimscribe: His Lives and Works*
1997: World Fantasy Award for Best Collection (nomination): *The Nightmare Factory*
1995: Bram Stoker Award for Best Short Fiction (nomination): *The Bungalow House*
1996: Bram Stoker Award for Best Fiction Collection: *The Nightmare Factory*
1996: Bram Stoker Award for Best Long Fiction: *The Red Tower*
2002: Bram Stoker Award for Best Long Fiction: *My Work Is Not Yet Done*
2002: International Horror Guild Award, Long Form Category: *My Work Is Not Yet Done*

"In broad strokes, *The Reckoning* declares that wars have a life of their own, even after we've forgotten about them. War is a ghost that comes back to haunt us long after we thought it was buried."

—*Jeff Long*

The Descent: Jeff Long
by Michael McCarty and Cristopher DeRose

Novelist Jeff Long's passion for climbing mountains and traveling to exotic locales has been entertaining readers for years. While he has also written the nonfiction books Outlaw: The True Story of Claude Dallas *and* Duel of Eagles: The Mexican and U.S. Fight for the Alamo, *he is no stranger to the dark side of speculative literature, having penned such thrillers as* The Ascent, *which was inspired by his 1977 stint in a Nepalese prison in a cell shared with the legendary wild men of the Mustang region above Annapurna. He also wrote the thought-provoking ghost story* The Reckoning, *explored the complexities of primal horror in* The Wall, *and dipped into an exploration of hell itself in* The Descent.

A self-described "oil rig brat," Jeff spent his early years traveling from state to state, eventually landing in Colorado, where he learned how to shoot, fashion belts from rattlesnake hide and was witness to nighttime apparitions, something that would seem to help him in his writing. A novelist, nonfiction writer, historian, journalist, screenwriter and natural risk-taker, Jeff climbed such mountains as Everest and Makalu.

His books have won several awards including the Texas Literary Award, the Western Writers of America Spur Award for Best Novel, the British Boardman-

Tasker Award for Mountain Literature and the American Alpine's Club Literary Award. His real-life adventures don't compare to the adventures of the mind that his books have taking readers on for over two decades, beginning with his debut novel Angels of Light (1987). Jeff's website is www.jefflongbooks.com.

Climbers can be a superstitious bunch. What are some of yours?

Keep your flip-flops and shoe soles down on the floor, never tipped (I learned that one in Nepal). Never step over someone's legs (Tibet). Never, ever touch the head of a monk (detonates your karma). Always try to have an extra pair of dry socks (expedition habit). If possible, walk clockwise around just about anything (chortens, cows lying in the road, sacred mountains). Don't ride shotgun in countries with landmine problems (the front and outside seat usually takes the brunt of any explosion). Keep your knots tight (shoelaces, climbing harness, anchor knots). And the number thirteen is lucky (at least it works for me).

Which came first: your love of suspense-horror, or climbing?

Nineteen sixty-three was my banner year for both; that was the year Americans first reached the summit of Mt. Everest which totally enthralled me. I was in seventh grade. Around the same time, I bought my first book, a paperback edition of *Dracula*. The Everest event infected me for life. The Dracula event forced me to sleep with a wooden crucifix on my chest until halfway through eighth grade. The two converged years later when I was soloing a wall called the Diamond. Halfway up, I spent the night in a hammock. Midnight came, and with it a vampire,

Author and adventurer Jeff Long in Mustang, a remote section of Nepal which he describes as "awesomely beautiful, a cross between Mars and the Grand Canyon and *Lost Horizon*" (photograph taken by Loba, a Mustang girl, in 2007).

his nails scratching on the rock. I even felt him/her clawing at my hammock, and knew for a fact I wouldn't make it until dawn. But I made it (at least I think I did), and by the light of day, I figured out that my night visitor had been mice that live in the cracks up there.

Year Zero is about the search for historical Jesus. Did your religious convictions strengthen or weaken when writing this novel?

According to some evangelicals who took the time to correspond with me, I have no religious convictions. In fact, I took on the historical Jesus after setting out to find the historical Satan [in *The Descent*]. Both are wildly fertile characters, especially if you try to set them in a real-life context. Long ago, while writing a history of the Alamo battle [*Duel of Eagles*], I learned that nothing makes a character more poignant than his or her warts and clay feet. When you can connect to a protagonist — god or not (and in Texas, Davy Crockett is a god) — at a gritty, personal level, then you rise above a reader's natural voyeurism and begin to feel and taste their suffering, sacrifices, and joys. That's the writer's biggest challenge, making a character really come alive.

How do you define "Fiction in High Definition"?

I sometimes wonder how many other writers actually listen to their readers. Certainly I do. This isn't the first time I've been asked what the hell "Fiction in High Definition" means, and had to fake an answer. To be honest, I can't remember what the hell "Fiction in High Definition" meant in the first place. So I've changed it on my website to "Extreme Fiction," because I usually write about the edge of the abyss.

Since you wrote a book with the same title, what did you think of the movie *The Descent*?

I'm still astonished by the identical elements, story setup, title, and monsters. Isn't one advised to be flattered in such circumstances? Or hire a lawyer? All I can imagine is that the director-writer, who keeps howling that there are no similarities, must have drunk too much warm English beer.

Why did you decide to write about Hell in *The Descent*?

Back in my all-boy Catholic high school, I was introduced to Dante's *Inferno* by Brother Bernard. He was a Golden Gloves champion who brooked no silliness, and freely powdered offenders with the chalkboard eraser thrown with amazing velocity and precision. I was desperately trying to stay awake — either during Brother Bernard's lecture about Dante's *Inferno*, or was it in a Franciscan monastery in northern New Mexico? — when my eye fell upon a crack in the floor. One thing led to another, and suddenly I found myself constructing an expedition into the circles of Hell. Years later, following the publication of my Everest novel [*The Ascent*], I was groping for a next topic to write about. I saw *The Ascent* on a bookshelf, upside down, and that instantly suggested *The Descent*. In the same instant, my Hell expedition came swarming up in Technicolor.

Was Satan modeled after anyone in *The Descent*?

No. Other characters were, though. If Dante could consign his enemies to various circles of eternal suffering, then I decided, why shouldn't I do the same? I only hope my enemies recognize themselves getting skewered, roasted, and served up. By the way, I'm adding to Dante's circles a special spot in Hell for plagiarists.

Were you influenced by Dante's *Inferno* in *The Descent*?

That and Jules Verne's *Journey to the Center of the Earth*, H.G. Wells's *The Time Machine* and Jorge Luis Borges' *The Circular Labyrinth*. Hell's a wonderful place to visit.

Who is more monstrous in *The Descent*, the humans or the monsters?

That's the question I'm asking throughout my *Descent* trilogy. Most of your stock Hollywood monsters are just animals with an appetite for humans. They're grizzly bears or man-eating lions dressed up as aliens or predators. But a bear isn't evil, it's just doing what bears do, though I have to say, one of the greatest horror movies in recent time was Herzog's *Grizzly Man*. My mission in the trilogy is to probe for deep horror and true monstrosity. In my hunt for the Devil, I'm asking if pure evil exists.

In the first book of the trilogy, *The Descent*, my answer to the question of pure evil is no, that pure evil is relative and a shared responsibility. I kill off the leader of the subterranean hominids, the historical Satan who rules Hell's monsters. At least he's the character we presume to be Satan, and that seems to be the end of it. *The Descent* is basically a Western horror — Western, as in our conquest of the frontier. Just as we came to admit the humanity of the *red devils* over time, *The Descent* exposes recognizable bits and pieces of the monsters' sameness with us, or our sameness with them.

But in my second and third books of the *Descent* trilogy, I'm exploring monstrosity at a whole other level. The monsters of *The Descent* have been largely exterminated, and a different kind of monster emerges. A real fallen angel exists. If there is such a thing as pure evil, it must reside in him, so the myths go. In *Deeper*, the second book, the angel is holed up in a subterranean chamber, something like bin Laden in his mountain cave. Now I get to have a dialogue with the ultimate villain. I mean to find out what makes him tick, and whether or not monsters can be more monstrous than we are.

The third book in the *Descent* trilogy will be called *Deliverance*, with a monumental tip of the hat to James Dickey. It picks up the story, landscape and two characters about ten years after *The Descent*. In the first book, we go down to find "them." In the second book, "they" come up after we wrote them off as an extinct species. The "fallen" angel — call him Satan, Santa, or Joe — makes his real debut in *Deeper*. Human virtues and vices get another workout in the search for missing children. At the center is a question I pondered in *The Descent* and will continue to ponder through *Deliverance,* and that is, "What is the face of God?"

The Reckoning can be seen as having a rather ambiguous narrative. It may or may not have a happy ending, or instance. Is there a definitive ending?

Yes. In broad strokes, *The Reckoning* declares that wars have a life of their own, even after we've forgotten about them. War is a ghost that comes back to haunt us long after we thought it was buried.

The Reckoning was also a search book, a search for an American pilot in Cambodia. Did you get any feedback from Vietnam veterans?

I consulted a colonel with the military unit that went into Cambodia during the Vietnam War, and fictionalized that unit and events. I also consulted with JPAC, the official military "archangel" which continues to search for the missing soldiers of past American wars. Several close friends were Vietnam vets, and helped me with details.

What was the inspiration for *The Reckoning*?

Back in 1992, I visited a friend with the U.N. in Cambodia. The Khmer Rouge were still active in the west, but we decided to chance a visit to Angkor Wat. Not too surprisingly, the place was empty, not a Westerner anywhere. Gunfire crackled in the far distance. There were a few monks and forest children, plus these solitary, sticklike survivors of the camps who wandered through the ruins like ghosts. It was a powerful stage for a ghost story. But I felt the story needed characters that American readers could relate to, and that defied me for another few years. Then I heard about a forensic unit with the U.S. military. Their mission is to find the remains of missing soldiers from past wars, particularly the Vietnam War, and that included digs in Cambodia. What if, I wondered, my ghosts were searching for their own remains? What if they had no idea they were ghosts? The story took off from there.

The Vietnam War is long over, but in *The Reckoning* the horrors persist. Why?

History is the biggest haunted house of them all. The Vietnam War helped shape my whole generation, and our children's, too, even if the children have no memory of it. But wars have a way of unleashing strange ghosts and demons long after the fact. They call to us. They demand our memory of them. Think about the power of the Missing in Action lobby, back before 9/11. It wasn't just the MIA families that were haunted. To one degree or another, we were all captive to impossible hopes and memories. It was true with Vietnam and, in a few years, it will be true with Iraq and Afghanistan. We don't own our wars. Wars own us.

Are there any plans to adapt any of your works to film?

My first book, *Outlaw*, a nonfiction account of a double homicide, was made into a CBS-TV movie back in 1985 by Jerry London, who did *Shogun*. Ted Talley, who won an Oscar for his adaptation of *Silence of the Lambs*, has written a powerful screenplay of *The Reckoning* for Reese Witherspoon and Paramount. David Goyer, who wrote *Batman Begins*, adapted *The Descent* for film (the real film has yet to be made). My novel *Angels of Light* was plagiarized and turned into *Cliffhanger*. I settled out of court. *Duel of Eagles* provided source material for a feature about the Alamo. I wrote a screenplay for Steven Seagal based on *The Ascent* and my article "The Silver Chalice," about my time in Nepal jails with CIA-trained Tibetan guerrillas. I just finished a script of *The Wall* for an independent director. Every one of my books has been optioned at some point in time.

What made you write *Duel of Eagles*?

Two things: First, I was born in Texas, and wanted to connect some circles. And second, I was inspired by Evan Connell's *Son of the Morning Star* about Custer and the Last Stand. It was incredibly fine history written with a novelist's palette, and furthermore written after whole bookshelves of other works on the man and the battle. When I first began researching, my goal was merely a better told version of the same old tale. But as I quickly discovered, there was an entirely different reality to the myth. Davy Crockett very probably surrendered and was executed. Travis took liquid mercury as a medicine for his syphilis, and was possibly insane. Jim Bowie was a brutal slave runner. Above all, the battle that has come to exemplify national defense (with its line in the sand) was, in fact, part of an American invasion of Mexico that didn't end until we had taken two-fifths of Mexico as part of our Manifest Destiny.

Have any of your books creeped you out?

I've tried to invest all of my recent books with the best demons and most creative horror I can. *The Descent* is full of the darkest savagery I could conjure. *Year Zero* was my take on the American Apocalypse. *The Wall* opens with a 3,000-foot fall off of El Cap and tapped into my vampire-on-the-Diamond experience, plus the natural dread of climbing. *Deeper* plunges into the old abyss. Whatever I've feared, I try to confront on the page.

If you could be any monster, which monster would you be?
The fallen angel. He's seen it all, including the face of God.

Books by Jeff Long

FICTION

Deeper (2007)
The Wall (2006)
The Reckoning (2004)
Year Zero (2002)
The Descent (1999)
Empire of Bones (1993)
The Ascent (1992)
Angels of Light (1987)

NONFICTION

Duel of Eagles: The Mexican and U.S. Fight for the Alamo (1990)
Outlaw (1984)

Awards

1991 — Texas Literary Award
1992 — Boardman-Tasker Mountain Literature Award
1992 — American Alpine Club Literary Award
1993 — Western Writers of America — Spur Award for Best Novel
2007   Banff Mountain Festival — Grand Prize

"I think it's all about tension and recognizing the absurd. Laughter is a way of relieving tension, and being in a horrifying situation can certainly be fraught with tension, but there's also the recognition of just how absurd it is, for example, to be trapped inside a shopping mall by a bunch of brain-eating animated corpses. You have to laugh."

— *Christopher Moore*

A Dirty Job: Christopher Moore

Raised on the works of Ray Bradbury, Richard Matheson, Kurt Vonnegut, Bram Stoker and John Steinbeck, San Francisco comic horror writer Christopher Moore has been writing international and New York Times best sellers. Besides getting rave reviews, he has established a loyal cult following.

After reading Douglas Adams' A Hitchhikers' Guide to the Galaxy, *Moore figured he could do the same thing Adams did, but instead of science fiction and satire, he would combine horror and zonked-out humor to create highly entertaining books.*

Moore was born in Toledo, Ohio, and grew up in Mansfield, Ohio. His father was a highway patrolman and his mother sold major appliances at a department store. He attended Ohio State University and Brooks Institute of Photography in Santa Barbara. He burst onto the scene with Practical Demonkeeping *(1992), a road adventure with an odd couple that gets odder: a 100-year-old seminarian named Travis O'Hearn and a green demon named Catch who has the nasty habit of eating most of the people he encounters.*

Moore's ten novels covered a wide spectrum of creatures including vampires, trickster gods, death merchants, sea monsters and stupid angels. He is the author of the books A Dirty Job; Island of the Sequined Love Nuns; The Lust Lizard of Melancholy Cove; Lamb: The Gospel According to Biff, Christ's Childhood Pal; Fluke: Or, I Know Why the Winged Whale Sings; *and* You Suck.

His latest novels are Fool, *a bawdy and perplexing tragic comedy based upon*

William Shakespeare's King Lear *but told through the eyes of the Fool, and* Bite Me, *the third book in the San Francisco Vampire Trilogy. Moore's websites are www.chrismoore.com and www.myspace.com/authorguy.*

Regarding *The Stupidest Angel*, were any of these works influential to you?:
A. "Gif of the Magi" by O. Henry,
B. *Night of the Living Dead* and
C. *Return of the Living Dead.*

As for the "Gift of the Magi," I actually used that plot, or a version of it, in *The Stupid Angel.* The other two were less influential. I think the scene from *Living Dead*, where the survivors are barricaded in a house, has sort of become iconic in zombie films and stories so I'm not sure if that counts as an influence or not. I suppose, indirectly, it does.

The Stupidest Angel had cuss words, cannibalism and people in their forties having sex. Do you believe the combination of all three is what Christmas is all about?

Horror and fantasy funny man Christopher Moore has plenty to smile about (photographed by Charlee Rodgers, 2002).

We put a stuffed fruitbat on our tree every year instead of an angel, and my girlfriend is half–Jewish, so we also have a menorah with Christmas lights in it. So my take on Christmas may be a little untraditional. While I don't think you have to have cannibalism and zombies to make for a perfect Christmas, I think it all helps.

Kurt Vonnegut recently passed away. Did you ever meet him?

I never met Kurt, but I always admired his work. I liked *Bluebeard* and *Galapagos* the best. The former because it gave me a grasp on what abstract expressionist painting was about, and the latter because of the "big brain" theory, equating our big brains with the saber-tooth tiger's teeth. It was brilliant. The form in *Bluebeard* was extraordinary as well: the short pieces that add up to a novel. He says you can arrange them in any order and they end up with the same effect. I haven't tried it, but it's still extraordinary just to attempt something like that.

Your mother died and your girlfriend's mother Charlee Rodgers also died before you wrote *A Dirty Job*. Was it hard to find humor after losing your own mother or was the book cathartic for you to write?

Actually, humor is how I deal with things, and the more dire, the more I'm tempted to crack wise. Charlee is the same way. We met during a flood in the small town where I used to live. We both had friends who had businesses on the main street, and the water was rising fast and they were trying to get their stuff to high ground. It was two in the morning and everyone was wading around, carrying cases of wine and whatnot, and Charlee and I were both joking and cracking up. I was all, "Hey, I can hang with this girl." So when our mothers died, I don't think I lost the sense of the absurd and the funny even during the events. Of course it was somber and sad at times, too, but even in the back of my mind I was taking notes, thinking about what I could bring to a story about death.

In *A Dirty Job*, Charlie Asher goes around collecting souls, and encounters a beautiful young woman whose soul is in her breast implants. If Charlie was in some place like Omaha, do you think he'd have the same problem?

Yes, I think that he might have encountered that in Omaha, although it's less likely. Vanity, however, isn't confined to the coasts. I have a friend who flew to Oklahoma City from Los Angeles for hair transplants. He researched it and said that that doctor was the best. I've been to Oklahoma City, and just being there would seem to take the edge off male pattern baldness. I mean, you can wear a hat until you get the hell out of Oklahoma City — then do something about your hair.

Also in *A Dirty Job*, Charlie's daughter Sophie can just point at people and say the word "kitty" and they would end up pushing daisies. Why the word "kitty"?

I just thought it would be funny. Also, *kitty* is one of those words that little kids identify, then name everything, like fire truck. You know, the little boy points to a fire truck and says "fire tuck" and the parents ooh and aah, then the kid points to Grandma and says "fire tuck" and they realize he's not the genius child they had hoped. I've thought about a second book with the Death Merchants, but I'm not sure where I'd start. I think I need to ponder it a bit.

Why do you think horror and humor go together so well?

I think it's all about tension and recognizing the absurd. Laughter is a way of relieving tension, and being in a horrifying situation can certainly be fraught with tension, but there's also the recognition of just how absurd it is, for example, to be trapped inside a shopping mall by a bunch of brain-eating animated corpses. You have to laugh.

Who is the next Christopher Moore?

I don't know. I mean, I'm not sure who the current Christopher Moore is. There are a lot of talented young writers out there sort of combining supernatural elements with humor, but I think they'll find their own niche, be their own person if they make it. I mean, I've been compared to Tom Robbins, Douglas Adams, and Kurt Vonnegut, and I'm honored to be mentioned in the same sentence with them but I don't write anything like those guys. The thing we have in common is that no one is sure what any of us is or was doing, and our stuff was funny. So the next writer to put on the goofy mantle will be his or her own person, carving out his or her own niche. That said, there's a guy named A. Lee Martinez, out of Texas, I think. I read his first book, *Gil's All Fright Diner*, and it shows great potential. I haven't read his other books, but he seems to have something going on with this horror-humor thing.

You have your email BSFiends@aol.com at the back of your books. Do you receive a lot of email?

I put that on my book *Bloodsucking Fiends*, back in '95, before my publisher was sending me on national tours, just so I could have some contact with my readers. I get anywhere from 50 to 100 emails a day from readers and I try to answer all of them. Obviously, because I need to get my writing done as well, the answers can be pretty short, but I really make an effort to touch base with my readers. Writing, like any art, is about communication, and I think communication should be a two-way thing.

The Internet is a huge time suck. And if I write a blog, for instance, my brain tells me that my writing is done for the day and I can't come up with anything for the current book. I think I have a mild case of Crow Syndrome, which I define as being somewhat like ADD, except you're susceptible to distraction by anything shiny. With the Internet, you're only a click away from the next shiny thing.

You've done a number of books set in your fictional town of Pine Cove. What do you like more there: The Head of the Slug or Brine's Bait, Tackle, and Fine Wines?

I liked the uniqueness of Brine's better. The Slug is like any number of small town saloons, but Brine's, a place run by a gourmet Zen fisherman, was something truly different. It was based on the general store in Cambria, California, which was owned by a guy who really did endeavor to carry the best in red worms, as well as fine wines, cheeses, freshly baked bread, and jumper cables. It's since turned into a more generic convenience store, but the original is preserved in fiction.

How many publishers saw *Practical Demonkeeping* before it was published?

Demonkeeping had already sold as a movie to Disney before it even went out to market in New York, so it wasn't out to market long with publishers. That said, I know it was rejected by a number of them and eventually picked up by St. Martins for a very modest advance. There was no frenzy about it the way there was with the film rights. And no, [the movie has] never been made and isn't even close.

What advice would you give to someone who just published their first novel?

Write another one. A better one. I mean, send query letters to agents and do all the stuff *The Writer's Market* tells you to do, but keep writing.

There are a number of characters who keep recurring in your books. Let's talk about what it is you like about each of these characters and if they were real, what you would say to them. Let's start with the Emperor.

The Emperor — I like that he's homeless and crazy, yet feels enormous empathy for the people of San Francisco, his subjects. If I met him, I suppose I'd give him some money and thank him for his concern.

Inspector Rivera.

He's a homicide inspector. I like that he has the ability to accept the high improbability of the situation he's in. In other words, if it looks like a vampire, and sounds like a vampire, the best way to deal with it is as if it's a vampire. He's tough and adaptable that way, yet not so self-assured that he doesn't question his own sanity at times. I don't know what I'd say to him. Maybe suggest he take a vacation somewhere.

Tommy Flood.

I like his earnest passion for life and the city. Tommy is based on me when I was nineteen, so it would be like talking to myself back in time. I guess I'd tell him to not lose a sense of what he wants to do, and warn him that it's going to take a lot of patience to get where he wants to go.

Jody.

Jody is just smoking hot — smart, pretty, funny, a little dangerous (the vampire thing does that). I like almost everything about her, but in the books, I like the way she finds her own power in the night, after realizing that she's always been just a wee bit afraid. If I met her, I guess I'd say, "Well, hello."

The Animals (turkey-bowlers).

These guys are based on the night crew I worked with in a grocery store when I was a kid. You have to love their ability to roll with the party, and find a celebration in every event. They're like a crew of not particularly dangerous pirates. I guess if I met them, I'd say, "Put the bong down and back away slowly, reality may hit you any moment."

Abby Normal.
Abby is all about the Goth girl voice. She's smart and very self-important, which makes her voice very funny. She passes judgment on everyone, despite having almost no experience to base her opinions on. I don't think I'd have anything to say to her; besides, she'd never hear it coming from a crusty dweeb like me.

Lily.
Lily is just Abby with a few more pounds on her. I like her sense of loyalty to Charlie, her boss, and her ability to go morose at the speed of dark. Again, I'm not really cool enough to talk to Lily.

Raziel.
Raziel is sort of like a golden Lab. He's very simple and literal, and seems to have no sense that he is this powerful, supernatural creature. Again, I'm not sure what I'd say to him. He's just, so, so, stupid.

Mavis Sand.
Mavis is the ultimate survivor, like a cockroach with a drinking problem, nothing short of nuclear war can kill her. She's been around, well, almost forever, and never seems to have a sense of what a hag she's become. I like that she's ancient, but still is kind of slutty. I don't think Mavis is the kind of person you "tell" anything to. I think you just ask questions.

Tucker Case and Roberto the Fruit Bat.
I like Tuck because he's a geek in a cool guy's body, and Roberto because he's a fruit bat. I think I'd tell Tuck he'd be a lot better person if he quit drinking and I'd tell Roberto to get off the Christmas tree.

Books by Christopher Moore

Practical Demonkeeping (1992)
Coyote Blue (1994)
Bloodsucking Fiends (1995)
Island of the Sequined Love Nuns (1997)
The Lust Lizard of Melancholy Cove (1999)
Lamb: The Gospel According to Biff, Christ's Childhood Pal (2002)
Fluke: Or, I Know Why the Winged Whale Sings (2003)
The Stupidest Angel; A Heartwarming Tale of Christmas Terror (2004)
A Dirty Job (2006)
You Suck (2007)
Fool (20009)
Bite Me (2010)

"Dracula is — all round — the best-ever monster character. Of the major monsters, he's unquestionably the most evil — none of that torn duality of Dr. Jekyll or the Wolf Man or the pathetic sufferings of the Frankenstein Monster, he's just an arrogant bastard with great dress sense, sexual charisma, enormous wealth, a castle (how cool is that?) and big plans. It helps in movies that he's the only monster who traditionally can hold a conversation with you as well as rip your throat out. The vampire myth is also open to all manner of varying interpretations that provide fertile material to the author or filmmaker, and so there's no end to ways of viewing the character."

— *Kim Newman*

The Night Mayor: Kim Newman

Kim Newman knows a lot about Dracula and vampires — and swears he isn't one of the undead. He is, however, a British writer who writes witty horror novels, alternate science fiction and dark fantasy books. He authored several nonfiction books as well and won numerous awards including the British Fantasy Award (seven times), the Bram Stoker (twice), the Hugo and the World Fantasy Award (three times).

His first novel, The Night Mayor, *tells the story of a computer-generated dream-world, a film noir virtual reality where two detectives try to track down a master criminal while dodging famous characters from movies. His other novels include* Bad Dreams, Life's Lottery, Jago, The Quorum *and the cult classic* Anno Dracula.

A film critic and journalist, Newman is well respected in the genres in England and the United States. To learn more about Newman, go to his website at www.johnnyalucard.com.

Ghastly Beyond Belief, the book you co-wrote with Neil Gaiman in 1985, a collection of quotations. Has the book ever been reprinted?

The book hasn't been reprinted, and no one has ever seriously asked. It'd probably have to be a facsimile edition, since the original is shot full of the sort of errors and glitches common to reference books of the pre–DVD, pre–Internet era. Though it was well liked, the book didn't exactly sell well (most of its tiny print run seems to have been shipped off to Australia like a boatload of convicts). Neil reports that several American publishers who were offered the book then responded along the lines of "I read the book while pissing myself laughing and then handed it around the office to all our other colleagues, who split their sides with hilarity until the paperback fell apart ... but there's no American market for it, so we're not making an offer."

Gaiman also wrote the introduction to your short story collection *The Original Dr. Shade & Other Stories*. Did you know that he was going to become as big as he did?

I know Neil's been disappointed to have worked so long and hard without any commercial or critical success, but he's a talented writer and I'm sure he'll gain a small devoted audience in the months following his death from starvation and neglect.

Why is horror and dark fantasy a good genre for you to write in?

As a critic, I spend a lot of time pigeonholing films into genres. For instance, the Danish Dogme manifesto rules out making genre movies, but I once went through the official list of Dogme films and pointed out which genre they belong to (Lars von Trier's *The Idiots* is a biker movie). As a fiction writer, I prefer to straddle genres. *Anno Dracula*, for instance, is a science fiction horror romantic historical crime mystery satire. I wrote a few more-or-less straight horror novels and stories (*Bad Dreams*, *Jago*) but have been doing more mix-and-match general weirdness since then.

You've written *Doctor Who* and the Doctor Who novella *Time & Relative*. Why do you think this series has been so popular for over four decades?

Eccentricity, and the amazingly versatile premise. It's a show that can literally go anywhere and encompass anything. Its occasional dips all come about when it becomes too tied up with its own history and continuity.

How are American horror fiction and movies different from the British?

Both countries have rich and varied horror scenes in both media, so it's hard to draw generalizations. You could argue that British horror is more sophisticated and literary and American horror is all guts and splat, but Peter Straub is American and James Herbert is British.

Was your short story collection *Famous Monsters* a tribute to Forry J Ackerman and the *Famous Monsters of Filmland* magazine?

The reference is obviously there and explicit in the story. Though I wasn't a great *Famous Monsters* reader as a kid. By the time I was interested in films, I thought the magazine was too childish and tacky and preferred the books which were starting to appear from critics like Carlos Clarens, David Pirie,

John Baxter, Philip Strick and Ivan Butler, which offered more than synopses and illustrations.

Your books have been translated into numerous languages and are read all over the world. Do you need to keep that international audience in mind as you write?

I barely keep a national audience in mind. I try to write in the interests of the story rather than any national reader.

You are a big fan of H.G. Wells. If Wells was alive today, would he be a science fiction novelist or a science fiction screenwriter?

Neither — he'd have hated being categorized as a genre writer, and would have wanted the sort of critical or publicity treatment J.G. Ballard, Martin Amis or Salman Rushdie get rather than being shoved out in paperback with a spaceship on the cover. He was among the first writers seriously to be interested in screenwriting, directed what we might now call underground films (self-financed and experimental) and got the deluxe treatment (with mixed results) on *Things to Come*. If he were around today, I think he'd want to front those Simon Schama–type 12-part documentary historical-scientific-political TV epics (though his squeaky Cockney voice would still be a handicap). In the 1890s, after *The Time Machine* was published, he collaborated with a British film pioneer on patents for what we'd now recognize as a theme park ride: Patrons would sit in a replica time machine and films would run on the wall and ceiling to simulate traveling through time. He was obsessed with tabletop war games, too, so he might be more interested in designing computer games or interac-

Kim Newman in London (photograph by Maura McHugh, 2006).

tive media than conventional novel-writing (a field he abandoned surprisingly early in his career — the later books are mostly tracts rather than proper fiction).

In you short story collection ***Seven Stars***, the story "Angel Down, Sussex" has Aleister Crowley and Sir Arthur Conan Doyle mixed up with a UFO sighting and psychic shapeshifters. Why did you pair up Crowley and Doyle for that story?

They were roughly contemporaries, and both interested in what we now call Fortean phenomena — plus they were both big, interesting, blustering characters and great fun to write about. Off the top of my head, I've no idea if they ever met, but they must have known about each other. Crowley actually wrote some detective short stories, so he presumably read his Holmes. It would have been unusual if he hadn't.

What was your inspiration for *Anno Dracula*?

Here's how *Anno Dracula* evolved. At Sussex University in 1978, I took a course entitled Late Victorian Revolt, taught by the poet Laurence Lerner and Wells' biographer Norman Mackenzie. I wrote a thesis, "The Secular Apocalypse: The End of the World in Turn of the Century Fictions," which later cropped up as the work of the main character of my third novel, *Jago*. For the thesis, I read up on invasion narratives (George Chesney's *The Battle of Dorking*, Wells' *The War in the Air*, Saki's "When William Came"), which imagine England overwhelmed by its enemies (usually the Germans). I was already interested in alternate-history science fiction, and recognized in these mostly forgotten stories the precursors of the many 20th-century stories which imagine an alternative outcome to World War II featuring a Nazi occupation of Britain (Len Deighton's *SS/GB*, Kevin Brownlow's film *It Happened Here*). In a footnote to my section on invasions, I described Dracula's campaign of conquest in Stoker's 1897 novel as "a one-man invasion."

I'm not sure when all the connections were made, but at some point in the early '80s it occurred to me that there might be story potential in an alternative outcome in which Dracula defeats his enemies and fulfills his stated intention to conquer Britain. It still seems to me something of a disappointment that Stoker's villain, after all his meticulous planning and with five hundred years of scheming monstrousness under his cloak, has no sooner arrived in Britain than he trips up and sows the seeds of his eventual undoing by an unlikely pursuit of the wife of a provincial solicitor. Van Helsing describes Dracula's project in Britain as to become "the father or furthurer of a new order of beings, whose road must lead through Death, not Life." Yet Stoker allegorizes Dracula's assault on Britain entirely as an attack on the Victorian family, an emblem of all the things he prized and saw as fragile. It just struck me as an interesting avenue to explore the kind of England, the kind of world that would result if Van Helsing and his family of fearless vampire killers were defeated and Dracula was allowed to father and further his new order.

The idea lay about in my head gathering dust, and the odd character, until Stephen Jones asked me to write something for an anthology project he was working on in 1991, *The Mammoth Book of Vampires*. Steve's request prompted me finally to set down the parameters for *Anno Dracula*, in that I felt a mammoth book of vampires should have some showing from the king of the undead. The result was *Red Reign*, which first appeared in Steve's book and is the bare skeleton of *Anno Dracula*. Meanwhile I'd already been drawn to vampires in my work under the name of Jack Yeovil for GW Books' tie-ins to their wholly owned *Warhammer* fantasy universe. As Jack, I developed not only a system of vampirism that, crossbred with Bram Stoker's, survives in the *Anno Dracula* novels, but also the creature who became their most popular character. For the record, the Geneviève of Yeovil's Drachenfels and Genevieve Undead (now collected with other material as *The Vampire Genevieve*) is not the same character as the Geneviève of *Anno Dracula*, but she is her trans-continual cousin.

For me, book ideas are like coral reefs, built up as bits and pieces stick together over years. With *Anno Dracula*, I had the background and the two lead characters — Charles Beauregard, who was intended as a dashing Victorian hero along the lines of Rudolph Rassendyll in *The Prisoner of Zenda* or Gerald Harper in the old TV series *Adam Adamant Lives!*, and the vampire girl Geneviève — plus the notion (probably inspired by Philip José Farmer) of a large cast list which would include not only real Victorians (Oscar Wilde, Gilbert and Sullivan, Swinburne) but famous characters from the fiction of the period (Raffles, Fu Manchu, various Holmesian hangers-on, Dr. Moreau, Dr. Jekyll). In *The Night Mayor*, my first novel, I had explored the idea of a consensus genre world, whereby all the faces and figures from 1940s films noirs hung out in the same city, and it was an obvious step to make the London of *Anno Dracula* a similar site, where the criss-crossing stories of all the great late Victorian horror, crime and social melodramas were being played out at the same time. This adds to a certain spot-the-reference feel some readers have found annoying but which others really enjoy. I admit to getting a tiny thrill when I can borrow a character from E.M. Forster (Henry Wilcox, from *Howard's End*) or resurrect someone as forgotten as Guy Boothby's Moriarty-esque mastermind Dr. Nikola. This also allows me to make the novel as much a playground as a minefield, and to go beyond historical accuracy to evoke all those gaslit, fogbound London romances.

One of the things my plot needed was a plethora of vampires, since Dracula would have turned a great many Britishers into his get, starting with a couple of Stoker's characters (Arthur Holmwood, Mina Harker) and extending to a lot of real people from Queen Victoria to a horde of walk-on prostitutes and policemen. I decided that if Dracula were to replace Prince Albert as Victoria's consort, then all the other vampires of literature would come out of hiding and flock to his court in the hope of advancement. After Dracula, the best-known vampire in literature is Dr. Polidori's Byronesque Lord Ruthven, and so he came forward to take the job of Dracula's prime minister and stick around for the rest of the Lord Ruthven. I decided to let Le Fanu's Carmilla stay dead, but at least gave her a mention, and thought it obligatory to have some fun at the expense of the real-life Elizabeth Bathory (my version owes more to Delphine Seyrig in *Le Rouge aux levres* than history) and Anne Rice's Lestat (a fashion leader for clothes-conscious vampires). I enjoyed cramming in as many previous vampires as possible, to the extent of writing a speech which finds Ruthven nastily listing all his peers and being rude about them. In the follow-up novels, I have enjoyed working a bit more with Les Daniels' Don Sebastian de Villanueva and Barbara Steele's Princess Asa Vajda, but I am wary of doing too much with other people's characters when the original creators might not yet be finished with them.

The final element that dropped into place, enabling me to write a draft of *Red Reign* very quickly, was the actual plot. I needed a genuine spine for the story, which would enable me to explore the world I had created, and I wanted something that would take the readers on a tour of my London that would include the slums and the palaces. The story of Jack the Ripper would have been hard to keep out of *Anno Dracula*, but I got the idea that the unknown serial killer was a vampire (a theme Robert Bloch made his own in "Yours Truly, Jack the Ripper" and which has been rehashed several times since) not only struck me as old hat but also not quite right for a story in which vampires were out in the open rather than cowering in the fog. So, with the world turned upside down, it became clear that Jack the Ripper should be a vampire killer; Stoker had obligingly called one of Van Helsing's disciples Jack, made him a doctor and indicated that his experiences in the novel were pretty much pushing him over the edge. Therefore, Stoker's Dr. Seward became my Jack the Ripper, driven mad by the staking of Lucy Westenra, with whom he was in love, and stalking vampire whores in Whitechapel. (To make his situation more complex, I made Mary Kelly, the Ripper's last victim, the get of the vampire Lucy and also her near-lookalike.)

The Ripper story is nowadays almost as big a favorite with the conspiracy theorists as the Kennedy assassination, and so it became quite natural to depict the effects of a series of sex crimes on a volatile society. With a killer on the loose, my other characters had all sorts of reasons — self-serving or noble — to find out who he was, to hinder or help his crimes or to make propagandist use of him. I was trying, without being too solemn, to mix things I felt about the 1980s, when the British government made "Victorian Values" a slogan, with the real and imagined 1880s, when blood was flowing in the fog and there was widespread social unrest. The Ripper murders also gave the novel a structure. The real dates of the killings — I couldn't resist adding the Ripper's most famous fictional victim, Wedekind's Lulu, to his historical list — became pegs for the plot, and other actual events like a Bernard Shaw speech, the bogus letters from the Ripper to the press or an inquest also fit surprisingly well into the fantasy. In reworking history, I took as a starting point Stoker's imagined world rather than our own, even to the extent of finally presenting to the public Kate Reed, a character conceived by Stoker for *Dracula* but omitted from the novel (and who has become more important in the sequels). I realized early on that there was enough in the world to merit return visits. I didn't especially want to do a direct sequel, since the last chapter of *Anno Dracula* more or less indicates what is about to happen in the country and how our main characters will be involved in it. However, vampires live long lifetimes and it was clear that the events of *Anno Dracula* would resonate well into the 20th century, which gave me room for more stories.

I've written two further novels, *The Bloody Red Baron*, set during the first world war, and *Dracula Cha Cha Cha*, set in Rome in 1959. I've also done a series of novellas set from 1945 to 1989 (so far), which will eventually become a fourth book, *Johnny Alucard*, and maybe even a fifth. I once planned to do a side story about a vampire Billy the Kid, spinning off from a brief mention in *Anno Dracula*, but I'm less inclined to do that since the idea was usurped by the schlock filmmaker Uwe Boll for *BloodRayne 2*.

You also wrote ***Andy Warhol's Dracula*** **(*Blood for Dracula*). Why do you think the count is still going strong after over a century?**

Dracula is — all round — the best-ever monster character. Of the major monsters, he's unquestionably the most evil — none of that torn duality of Dr. Jekyll or the Wolf Man or the pathetic sufferings of the Frankenstein Monster, he's just an arrogant bastard with great dress sense, sexual charisma, enormous wealth, a castle (how cool is that?) and big plans. It helps in movies that he's the only monster who traditionally can hold a conversation with you as well as rip your throat out. The vampire myth is also open to all manner of varying interpretations that provide fertile material to the author or filmmaker, and so there's no end to ways of viewing the character.

What are some of your favorite vampire books and movies?

Books — *Dracula, I Am Legend, Doctors Wear Scarlet, Throat Sprockets, The Empire of Fear, Carmilla, The Black Castle, The Golden*. Movies — *Nosferatu* (1922, 1979), *Dracula* (1931, 1958), *Let's Scare Jessica to Death, The Mask of Satan, Daughters of Darkness, Let the Right One In, The Addiction, Vampire Circus* (and most other Hammer vampire films), *The Night Stalker, Near Dark, Mr. Vampire.*

If you could be any monster, which monster would you be and why?

Dracula — see above. Not that keen on killing people, though.

What's next for you?

I'm working on "Cry-Babies," a Radio 4 play due to go out early in 2009, and am about to start a novella (which will probably become a chunk of a book) called *The Hound of the d'Urbervilles*. I'm committed to doing a third collection in the series which began with *The Man from the Diogenes Club* and *Secret Files of the Diogenes Club*.

Books by Kim Newman

FICTION

The Night Mayor (1989)
Bad Dreams (1990)
Jago (1991)
In Dreams co-edited Paul J. McAuley (1992)
Anno Dracula (1992)
The Quorum (1994)
The Original Dr. Shade and Other Stories (1994)
Famous Monsters (1995)
The Bloody Red Baron (1995)
Back to the USSA (1997)
Judgment of Tears: Anno Dracula 1959 (1998)
Andy Warhol's Dracula (1999)
Life's Lottery (1999)
Where the Bodies Are Buried (2000)
Seven Stars (2000)
Dracula Cha Cha Cha (2000)
Unforgivable Stories (2000)
Binary 2 (2000)
Time and Relative (2001)
Dead Travel Fast (2005)
The Man from the Diogenes Club (2006)
Secret Files of the Diogenes Club (2007)

NONFICTION

Ghastly Beyond Belief, co-written with Neil Gaiman (1985)
Horror: 100 Best Books, co-edited with Stephen Jones (1988)
Nightmare Movies: A Critical History of the Horror Film, 1968–88 (1985)

Wild West Movies: Or How the West Was Found, Won, Lost, Lied About, Filmed and Forgotten (1990)
BFI Companion to Horror (1996)
Millennium Movies: End of the World Cinema (1999)
Cat People (1999)
Apocalypse Movies: End of the World Cinema (2000)
Science Fiction/Horror: Sight and Sound Reader (2001)
Horror: Another 100 Best Books, co-edited with Stephen Jones (2005)
Horror: The Complete Guide to the Cinema of Fear, co-written with James Marriott (2005)
Doctor Who (2005)

Awards

1989: The Bram Stoker Award (presented by the Horror Writers of America) for "Best Non Fiction 1989." (*Horror: 100 Best Books*)
1990: British Science Fiction Award for "Best Short Fiction 1990" ("The Original Dr. Shade")
1992: The Children of the Night Award (presented by the Dracula Society) for "Best Novel 1992" (*Anno Dracula*)
1994: the Fiction Award of the Lord Ruthven Assembly for *Anno Dracula*
1994: the International Horror Critics' Guild Award for Best Novel for *Anno Dracula*
1998: the International Horror Guild Award (1997) for Best Long Fiction for "Coppola's Dracula."
1999: Prix Ozone for Foreign Fantastic Novel for *Anno Dracula* (France)
2001: British Fantasy Award for Best Collection 2000. The winning book was: *Where the Bodies Are Buried*, published by Alchemy Press.
2006: Bram Stoker Award for Best Non Fiction 2005 (*Horror: Another 100 Best Books*, co-edited with Stephen Jones).

He has also been short-listed for the following:
British Fantasy Award (seven times)
Bram Stoker Award in the "Best Novel" category
Hugo Award for the 2005 Prix Victor Hugo Awards Ceremony.
International Horror Guild Award in the Long Fiction, and Nonfiction categories.
Sidewise Award for Alternate History for *The Bloody Red Baron* (1995), "Abdication Street" (1996), "Teddy Bears Picnic" (1997), "The Other Side of Midnight" (2000), and the 2005 Prix Victor Hugo Awards Ceremony (2005).
World Fantasy Award (three times)

"The studio asked Dan Curtis to direct a film version [Burnt Offerings] of the novel, and Dan said "yes," and called me in to write the screenplay. We threw out the first section of the book (which was set in downtown New York) and started in the country when the family arrives at this haunted house. Most critics panned the film, but the public loved it. I happen to think it has some really scary scenes."
—*William F. Nolan*

From *Logan's Run* to London Bridge: William F. Nolan

With more than 83 books and some 750 magazine pieces to his credit, as well as having had his work selected for over 325 anthologies and textbooks, William F. Nolan is a one-man word factory. He has several other writing projects in the works, so keep your eyes out for even more from the legendary speculative fiction writer in the near future. Currently he is working on ten book projects including another Logan's Run *and Sam Space books,* Dark Universe *with Blue Water Comics and more.*

What's the story behind the unproduced script *The Night Killers*, written by you and Richard Matheson?

It was to become the third *Kolchak* Movie-of-the-Week. Dan Curtis asked me to write the first draft and set up the basic plot and characters. This was in late 1973 after he and Matheson had done *The Night Stalker* and *The Night Strangler*. I wrote the 100-page first draft in just seven days. The original story was mine. Then Matheson took it over for the final teleplay, adding and cutting. Curtis and the network okayed our final and we were all set for the shoot in Hawaii when we were informed that *Kolchak* had been sold as a weekly series. This killed our Movie-of-the-Week and, until last year with its inclusion in Gauntlet's publication of *Richard Matheson's The Kolchak Scripts*, our teleplay has remained buried. At least now people can see what it would have been like on the screen, had the script been produced as planned.

***The Norliss Tapes* was based on a story** by novelist Fred Mustard Stewart. How did the story and your screenplay differ?

I'm sure that I read the story outline by Stewart, but I can't recall it. It had something to do with a walking dead man. Beyond that, everything in the teleplay is mine. I wrote it without any references whatever to the Stewart story.

You did the 1974 adaptation of Henry James' *The Turn of the Screw* that was filmed in London with Lynn Redgrave. Was James' story easy or difficult to adapt?

Difficult, in that I had to "extend" the material from a novelette to a two-night miniseries. I wanted to retain the mood and period atmosphere and to remain faithful to James' concept and characters. Apparently I pulled it off, because the critical reception to my teleplay was very positive. It remains one of my best scripts.

What kind of research did you have to do on Machine Gun Kelly to write *Melvin Purvis: G-Man*?

Luckily, I own many books dealing with the gangster era of the 1930s, and I know quite a lot about those days, so it was no big deal to dig out some basic facts on Kelly. My version was largely fictional, anyhow. Dan let me play a bit in this one, which was shot up in the Sacramento area. I got to die on the roof of the gang's roadhouse in a hail of FBI bullets with a Tommy gun in

William F. Nolan (left) and author Michael McCarty (right) at the Evanston Library, Evanston, Illinois, during the World Horror Convention (photograph by Cindy McCarty, 2002).

my hands. I'd always wanted to fire a Thompson sub-machine gun and, even with blanks, it was a great experience.

Was *Kansas City Massacre* a sequel to *Melvin Purvis*?
Yes and no. It was produced as a direct follow-up Movie-of-the-Week since the network wanted to take advantage of the original. *Purvis* had topped the ratings. So I was asked to write the second one, which also did very well. The network wanted yet another, so I did an outline for Dan titled *The Great Dillinger Manhunt*, but it somehow never jelled. (By the way, John Dillinger was not killed by the FBI outside the Biograph in Chicago in 1934. A look-alike "patsy" was set up and killed so Dillinger could make his final escape. He retired from crime and died many years later in upper California.)

Karen Black starred in all three stories in the first *Trilogy of Terror*. Was that planned when the teleplay was written?
Yes, Dan wanted the same actress to star in all three tales. My two were totally eclipsed by Matheson's "Prey" featuring that evil little Zuni Fetish doll. That's the one that everyone remembers. It made a terrific impact. Karen Black was extraordinary in those multiple roles. Very impressive.

What are your thoughts on *Terror at London Bridge*?
I had always wanted to write a story about Jack the Ripper but the problem was to find a totally fresh approach. That problem was solved when my wife Cameron and I visited the London Bridge in Lake Havasu, Arizona. A wealthy American bought the bridge from England, had it torn apart and shipped over, stone by stone, to the U.S. They rebuilt it in Arizona and diverted a section of the Colorado River to run under it. When my wife and I arrived there, it was late at night and all the other tourists were gone. We were the only people in this British village built around the bridge. I stood there, looking up at the dark stone structure. Then I said, "I'll bet Jack the Ripper walked over this bridge after his murders in Whitechapel." And that did it. I had my fresh approach. My idea was that the Ripper had been shot on the bridge and had been crushed by a stone that fell with him into the river. It's found at the bottom of the Thames a century later and brought back to Arizona to be fitted into the structure and a drop of tourist's blood brings him "back" to start his reign of terror all over again. It worked out beautifully. Prime popcorn entertainment.

What was the story behind the movie *Burnt Offerings*?
The studio asked Dan Curtis to direct a film version of the novel, and Dan said "yes," and called me in to write the screenplay. We threw out the first section of the book (which was set in downtown New York) and started

in the country when the family arrives at this haunted house. Most critics panned the film, but the public loved it. I happen to think it has some really scary scenes. Last year Dan and I did an audio commentary for the DVD edition.

What led up to you, Matheson and Curtis working together again on *Trilogy of Terror 2*?

Richard Matheson had nothing to do with the second *Trilogy*. Dan simply re-shot Matheson's Bobbie from his earlier script and put it in as the middle story. Then Dan and I wrote the other two as a team. I had always wanted to have a crack at writing about the Zuni doll, since it was all anybody ever talked about from the first *Trilogy*, so it was very satisfying being able to do it at last.

I felt your two stories in *Trilogy of Terror 2* were even better than the original *Trilogy*.

I'd like to say I feel the same way, but it's not up to me to judge. I can't be objective about them. I did the best I could with the material at hand. In my opinion, the best segment of all would have been my adaptation of Philip K. Dick's "The Father-Thing" but it got dropped at the last moment and replaced with Matheson's "Bobbie." My Dick teleplay was very frightening, but no one ever got a chance to see it.

Curtis, who directed nine of your produced scripts, died in 2006. You and he worked so well together and he was a friend of yours as well. Can you give us a Dan Curtis anecdote?

Dan's death was a terrific shock to me. He was *so* full of life, a real dynamo. I can't believe he's gone. We were a great team. I worked on fifteen film-television projects with him over the years from *The Norliss Tapes* to *Trilogy of Terror II*. Alas, six of our planned projects (me as writer, with Dan producing and directing) never got made.

As for a Curtis anecdote: when we were shooting my teleplay *Melvin Purvis, G-Man* up in Sacramento, California, I played the minor role of a gangster that Purvis kills on the roof of a tavern. The scene went on and on, and finally I lifted my head to see if Curtis had finished shooting the scene. He had *not*. Dan yelled at me: "Nolan, damn you, keep your head down! You're supposed to be *dead*." We had a lot of laughs over that.

You say that you've written 19 unproduced scripts. What are some of the best of these?

That's a tough one to answer because I'm fond of all of them. Most people are not aware that in Hollywood, only about one of ten accepted scripts ever gets produced. The others are assigned, paid for, written in blood, and then, for one reason or another, put on the shelf. I worked my ass off on every one of my 19 unproduced scripts.

For *Murder on the Istanbul Train*, the network sent me overseas, where I rode this train across Europe into Vienna and turned in a really exciting script. But the actress who was to star in it, and for whom it was written, took on another project. My train was dead on the tracks. George Clayton Johnson and I sold an original half-hour teleplay, "Dreamflight," to Rod Serling at *The Twilight Zone*, but they went to hour scripts for the season and that was that. I wrote a neat, moody screenplay [*De Pompa*] for director Billy Friedkin (who flew me down to the Gulf of Mexico to scout locations), but before we could get it produced, Billy was off to New York to direct *The French Connection*. A producer at MGM called me in to write an action Western I called *The Nighthawk Rides!* They decided, once it was done, that it was "too close to Zorro," so it never got made. (It was later printed in *The Best of the West*.) The irony here is that they had originally asked for a "Zorro-like" script! Buck Houghton, who worked for Serling in producing *The Twilight Zone*, hired me to write the pilot for a new TV series, *Just Before Dark*, a clone of *Zone*, and I based the script on my oft-reprinted story "The Small World of Lewis Stillman." But the producer died before the cameras could turn.

And I've written before about the ill-fated story behind my two-night miniseries based on Peter Straub's "Floating Dragon." I spent six months adapting his novel, and finally had a shooting script everyone loved at NBC. It was greenlighted for production and just eight days before the first day of principal photography all of the execs at NBC were fired and their projects scrapped. End of the Dragon! I could go on with other sad tales about aborted scripts, but it's too painful. I must stop.

Just how serious are you as a scriptwriter? Do you try for depth and symbolism?

Basically I'm an entertainer, a storyteller. I'm not out to challenge Shakespeare. Whatever makes the story I'm telling work well for the screen is what I put into the scripts. I never deliberately try for depth and symbolism. If people find these elements in what I wrote for films or television, that's fine with me. But I never say to myself, "Ah, I'll make this scene deeper," or "Ah, I'll put in a symbol here." Whatever works best for the story, that's what concerns me.

What does the F. in William F. Nolan stand for?

The F. is for Francis, a name I've always disliked. Which is why I called the villain "Francis" in *Logan's Run*.

Is anything in the works at the moment?

It looks as if I'll be signing a contract for substantial option money (and a producer's slot) on my farout *Sam Space* series, about a tough private eye on Mars dealing with three-headed clients, etc. I won't believe it until I have the contract in my hands. I've been at this game far too long to believe in any deal until it actually happens. And, of course, Warner Bros. keeps telling me that they *are* going to remake *Logan's Run* as a megabuck production. Oh, no screenplay yet, but heck, they've only been on it for six and a half years! So we shall see what we shall see.

The Films and TV Works of William F. Nolan

A Dream of the Stars (1953) (Documentary)
Brain Wave (1959) ("One Step Beyond")*
Vanishing Act (1959) ("Wanted: Dead or Alive")*
Black Belt (1960) (Wanted: Dead or Alive")*
Down the Long Night (1960) (Episodic Series)
Assault on a Queen (1966) (Motion Picture)*
The Joy of Living (1971) ("Norman Corwin Presents")
The Harrad Experiment (1973) (Motion Picture)*
The Norliss Tapes (1973) (NBC TV Movie)
The Turn of the Screw (1974) (ABC 2-night Miniseries)
Melvin Purvis: G-Man (1974) (TV Movie)
Trilogy of Terror (1975) (ABC TV Movie)
The Kansas City Massacre (1975) (ABC TV Movie)
Sky Heist (1975) (NBC Movie of the Week)
Logan's Run (1976) (Motion Picture)
Burnt Offerings (1976) (Motion Picture)
Logan's Run (1977) (TV Pilot)
First Loss (1981) ("240-Robert")
The Partnership (1981) ("Darkroom")
The Thing (1982) (Motion Picture)*
Raymond Chandler's Los Angeles (1983) (Documentary)*
Terror at London Bridge (1985) (NBC Movie of the Week)
Such Interesting Neighbors (1986) (Anthology Series)*
Midnight's Child (1992) (TV Movie)*
Trilogy of Terror 2 (1996) (USA Movie of the Week)

*Uncredited works

Books by William F. Nolan

Ray Bradbury Review (1952) (Hardcover 1988)
A Cross-Section of Art in Science Fiction (1952)
Omnibus of Speed (1958) (co-edited with Charles Beaumont)
Adventures on Wheels (1959) (with John Fitch)
The Fiend in You (co-edited with Charles Beaumont)

Phil Hill — Yankee Champion (1962)
Impact 20 (1963) (Hardcover 2002)
Men of Thunder (1964)
When Engines Roar (1964) (Co-edited with Charles Beaumont)
John Huston: King Rebel (1965)
Sinners & Supermen (1965)
The Pseudo-People (1965) (Editor)
Man Against Tomorrow (1965) (Editor)
Logan's Run (1967) (co-written with George Clayton Johnson)
To the Highest Power (1968) (Editor/writer)
Death Is for Losers (1968)
The White Cad Cross-Up (1969)
Dashiell Hammett: A Casebook (1969)
A Wilderness of Stars (1969) (Editor)
A Sea of Space (1969) (Editor)
The Future Is Now (1970) (Editor)
The Human Equation (1971) (Editor/writer)
The Edge of Forever (1971) (Anonymously edited by Nolan)
Space for Hire (1971)
Steve McQueen: Star on Wheels (1972)
Alien Horizons (1974)
Hemingway: Last Days of the Lion (1974) (chapbook)
The Ray Bradbury Companion (1975)
Wonderworlds (1977) (published in the UK)
Logan's World (1977)
Logan's Search (1980)
Science Fiction Origins (1980) (co-edited with Martin H. Greenberg)
Max Brand's Best Western Stories (in 3 volumes: 1981, 1985, 1987) (Editor/Writer)
Hammett: A Life at the Edge (1983)
McQueen (1984)
Things Beyond Midnight (1984)
The Black Mask Boys (1985) (Editor/Writer)
Look Out for Space (1985)
Max Brand: Western Giant (1986)
The Work of Charles Beaumont (1986)
Logan: A Trilogy (1986)
Dark Encounters (1986) (chapbook)
The Work of William F. Nolan (1988)
Rio Renegades (writing as "Terrence Duncan") (1989)
Urban Horrors (1990) (co-edited with Martin H. Greenberg)
How to Write Horror Fiction (1990)
Blood Sky (1991) (chapbook)
The Bradbury Chronicles (1991) (co-edited with Martin H. Greenberg)
Helltracks (1991) (Paperback) (Hardcover 1999)
3 for Space (1992) (chapbook)
Helle on Wheels (1992) (chapbook)
The Black Mask Murders (1994)
Night Shapes (1995)
The Marble Orchard (1996)

The Brothers Challis (1996)
Tales of the Wild West (1997) (Editor)
Sharks Never Sleep (1998)
The Winchester Horror (1998)
Alone Tales of the Wild West (1999) (Editor)
California Sorcery (1999) (co-edited with William K. Schafer)
Down the Long Night (2000)
Logan's Return (2000) (internet book)
Dark Universe (2001)
Off-Beat (2002) (Editor)
Have You Seen the Wind? (2003)
With Marlowe in L.A. (2003)
The Logan Chronicles (2003)
Ships in the Night (2004)
Far Out (2004)
Nightworlds (2004)
Wild Galaxy (2005)
Demon! (2006)
Let's Get Creative (2006)
Masquerade (2007) (Editor)
Seven for Space (2007)
Nightshadows (2007)

Awards

William F. Nolan has won numerous awards. Here are some highlights:

Edgar Allan Poe Special Award for Mystery Writers of America
Bram Stoker Lifetime Achievement Award from the Horror Writers Association
"Cited for Excellence" by American Library Association
Author Emeritus by the Science Fiction Writers and Fantasy Writers of America
Living Legend in Dark Fantasy by the International Horror Guild
Golden Medallion television work at two European film festivals
Distinguished Career Away from the City of Los Angeles
Maltese Falcon Award from John Grill in San Francisco

"I'm interested in a lot of history and culture in general. The Napoleonic Wars are my personal favorite. But I am also interested in ancient Rome — that is a fascinating period. The history of China is something that I have become increasing interested in, as the result of writing the Temeraire books, because my character Temeraire is a Chinese dragon. That has drawn me into the vast history of China."

— *Naomi Novik*

Empire of Ivory: Naomi Novik
by Michael McCarty and Terrie Leigh Relf

Two thousand seven was a good year for fantasy novelist Naomi Novik. She won the Compton Crook and Locus Awards. Her fourth book in the Temeraire series, Empire of Ivory, was scheduled to be published on September 25 and she sold the film rights of her books to Peter Jackson, director of King Kong *and the* Lord of the Rings *trilogy.*

Her book His Majesty's Dragon *was the first in a seven-book series; the sequels are* Throne of Jade, Black Powder War, In the Service of the King, Empire of Ivory *and* Victory of Eagles.

Novik lives in New York City and is the daughter of Polish immigrants. She earned a degree in English Literature from Brown University, and a Masters in Computer Science with some post doctoral work in the same field. Also a "gamer," she is known for her work on the expansion of the Dungeons & Dragons computer game Neverwinter Nights: Shadows of Undrentide. *Her website is http://www.temeraire.org/.*

Did you originally intend *His Majesty's Dragon* to be a stand-alone novel or the first book in a series?

When I finished *His Majesty's Dragon*, I didn't have a contract yet. It was my first novel. I gave it to my agent Cynthia Manson and she sent it to editor Betsy Mitchell at Del Rey. I wasn't expecting to hear for quite a long time. That's what they tell you in all those writer's advice books. As I was waiting to hear from them, I knew I wanted to tell more stories about these characters, how their lives would go on. I was thinking of what I'd like to do when Del Rey called up and basically said they didn't want one book, they wanted more. I quickly put together a synopsis of the next two books for them. I had solid plans for seven books.

I generally like to be thinking a few books ahead as I write, so I can plan and do foreshadowing and give myself threads I can connect. It seems to happen organically; it's fun as a process. In a way, I do model on Patrick O'Brian's Aubrey/Maturin series, where it's the lives of these characters. I'd like to have each book to encompass a self-contained plot, even though I confess I ended *Empire of Ivory* on a sort of cliffhanger. The main plot was resolved within the book with a setup for the next book [*Victory of Eagles*]. I had to do it, I beg readers to forgive me for that one [*laughs*].

The Napoleonic Wars inspired you to write the Temeraire series of alternate history fantasy books.

I love the Napoleonic era in general for a long time. The Jane Austin books are set in that time period and the books by Patrick O'Brian [author of the nautical adventure classic *Master and Commander*] are big favorites of mine. I really love the flavor of the language. [I love] the comedy of manners and the social aspects combined with the swashbuckling adventure of the age itself.

On top of that, it is a good era for dragons. It's not the later, mechanized war, where you would have to start making dragons

Naomi Novik combines dragons and the high seas in fantasy books (photograph by Beth Gwinn, 2008).

almost unrealistically powered as biological creatures to be still dangerous without a lot of certain build-up. When you have anti-aircraft guns and airplanes in the air fighting against dragons, you can imagine that being interesting. I wanted the dragons to be believable, physical creatures in our world. You can still have this great interaction between an air force, ships and land battles. It really just sort of worked well.

Are you a history buff?

Yes I am. I'm interested in a lot of history and culture in general. The Napoleonic Wars are my personal favorite. But I am also interested in ancient Rome — that is a fascinating period. The history of China is something that I have become increasing interested in, as the result of writing the Temeraire books, because my character Temeraire is a Chinese dragon. That has drawn me into the vast history of China.

What can you tell us about the latest Temeraire book *Empire of Ivory*?

I don't want to give away too many spoilers. There is an excerpt from the first chapter of *Empire of Ivory* at the end of book three, which basically reveals what is going on in England while Captain Will Laurence [the series protagonist] and Temeraire have been away. They've been gone for about a year now; they were forced to travel to China, and they had to travel overland to come back. They got caught in one of the major campaigns of the Napoleonic Wars, the war where Napoleon basically beat the Prussians. On their way back, they have secured nothing from England. Once they come closer, they become very worried about why they haven't been hearing anything from England. They do reach England, at the start of *Empire of Ivory*. It is revealed that all the dragons in England are extremely sick with a disease, a kind of tuberculosis for dragons. It was brought over accidentally by a dragon shipped to England from America. All the dragons in England have this disease because it has infested all the different dragon communities, all the covert breeding grounds of England and British territories by the British courier dragons, because it wasn't realized how serious the disease was. They come back to England to find out all the other dragons are sick or dying. They have to find a cure.

Since you have considerable experience writing computer games, do you "see" your stories in-action while you write them?

I try to write my action scenes in a cinematic way. I try very hard to visualize exactly what is going on, so I can explain to the reader in three dimensions. Now that you mention it, my training in computer games definitely helps with that. I am certainly used to making characters move through space, which is something that not even necessarily watching movies gives you. Having to think about how characters are going to interact in a computer game definitely helps.

I wouldn't say that I think of it as a computer game while I'm doing it, but it is very much a concern of mine to make sure, if you are sitting there at home reading this scene trying to figure out how it's working, what is going on, that it is clear how these bodies are relating to each other.

Peter Jackson optioned your books for movies. Would you write the computer games for them?

Wow! If they asked me to, I'd certainly participate. Obviously, a computer game on that scale is never done by just one person. I'd be happy to look at a script or contribute to one. I'd be equally happy to see other people's interpretations and go on and write other novels. Either way is fine with me.

I'm not proprietary about the ideas and the concepts. I am having this wonderful experience right now that the foreign editions of my book have started to come in. I have these fantastic different covers coming in from all over the world. There were already the United States and the British editions, and now the British editions have a completely new style. It is really quite wonderful for me to see all these different interpretations of my work. I love the variety. I like mash-ups, when people put their own ideas on an existing pieces of work. I feel that is what happens with computer game rights and movie rights. You get to see what somebody else creates out of your work. I think that, in itself, is a really thrilling experience.

Has Jackson optioned just the first three books or future books, too?

He has optioned the first three books entirely and the rights to the series and the characters.

Have you been in contact with Jackson?

I have been in contact with Peter Jackson. I am not allowed to say anything whatsoever. Personally — options are for a quite a long period of time. I myself am not expecting anything to happen in the short run. Peter Jackson, Philippa Boyens, and Fran Walsh are still working on *The Lovely Bones* [based on the Alice Sebold bestseller]. I believe he has another project, *Avatar*. Peter Jackson has a lot of projects going on. I will get very excited when it becomes our turn, but until then, I don't really know, don't expect to know. I am resolutely putting it out of my mind [*laughs*].

You hear all these stories, of course, about how in Hollywood, things get optioned and nothing ever happens. I feel my work is done, my job is to be patient and let them do their work. I do think the creative process takes time. What you want is that it be done right and that is why I was so thrilled when I heard that Peter Jackson was interested. That tells me immediately that the project is going to be done right.

Do you find that your degree in British Literature added to your skill and creativity as a fiction writer?

Yes. I went to Brown University, which has the wonderful feature that there isn't any core curriculum. I actually did it in English Literature, so it is both British and American. Being old-fashioned, I preferred British. I studied a lot of Old English and Middle English literature in particular. I think that the abilities and skills I learned for analysis and an exposure to a wide range of literary traditions is really important for anyone who wants to be a writer. I was also able, because of the flexibility at Brown, to take a lot of science classes, biology, computer science, international relations, political science, and history classes — those kind of things. In no sort of prescribed order, the university allows you to pursue your interests and take the best classes in every discipline. That is about as good a training as you can get for any kind of creative profession. That broad exposure which is traditionally the idea of Liberal Arts, is something very valuable and has been very valuable to me.

Do you have any personal connections to dragons?

I think they are amazingly cool. Wawel has made a big impression. I'm Polish. One of the most famous legends of Poland, the founding of Poland, is the Wawel dragon. That is a legend I grew up with as a child. Outside Krakow, Poland, where the old palace used to be, there is a bronze statue of the Wawel dragon — it's quite modern and it breathes fire. That was something that was really fun for me to see when I was in Poland a few years ago.

You are a self-described "big geek and fan girl." Care to elaborate?

The first book my mother ever read to me was *The Hobbit*. I have a big, battered picture book from when I was about four or five, and I read *The Lord of the Rings* for the first time in first grade. I am sure I missed about nine-tenths of what was going on. That really is a start of a tradition of being a big fan of science fiction and the fantasy genre in general. That has led me, in a lot of ways, to being interested in computer science and programming. I am a fan of most of the science fiction and fantasy. Being a geek in certain ways is about having deep passions in weird areas and being able to follow them. That is very much what I am.

Books by Naomi Novik

SERIES

Temeraire
His Majesty's Dragon (2006)
Throne of Jade (2006)
Black Powder War (2006)

Laurence Arc
Empire of Ivory (2007)
Victory of Eagles (2008)
Tongues of Serpents (2010)

Awards

Compton Crook Award for Best First Novel (2006)
Locus Award for Best First Novel (2006)

"[Many breakthrough inventions] came out of science fiction. None of them took me by surprise, because I had been reading about them for years before they happened. I was in Paris in August 1945, and I was getting a haircut in a barber shop off the Chantier, Lisse. And I was looking over the shoulder of the man next to me, and he had a newspaper with a big headline, 'Le Bomb et Amique.' And the first thing I thought was that these crazy French will print anything in their papers. And then when I looked a little closer and realized it actually had happened. I felt, 'Well, I knew it all along,' and I had."
— *Frederik Pohl*

The Gateway Trip: Frederik Pohl

Frederik Pohl is often regarded as one of the greatest living science fiction writers. His name is synonymous with superb speculative fiction.

Pohl was born on November 26, 1919, in Brooklyn, New York. He fell in love with writing at an early age. "I wrote this poem for Amazing Stories *when I was fifteen," he recalled. "It was accepted when I was sixteen, published when I was seventeen and paid for when I was eighteen."*

His long career in science fiction stretches over seven decades. At age nineteen, he was editing two magazines, Astonishing Stories *and* Super Science Stories. *Pohl also edited* Galaxy, If *and* Worlds of Tomorrow. *He has written over 150 books, including such SF classics as* The Space Merchants, Gateway, Man Plus, Black Star Rising, The Day the Martians Came, The Voice of Heaven, Outnumber the Dead *and* Jem. *His recent works include* Chasing Science *and the three-part Eschaton Sequence (*The Other End of Time, The Siege of Eternity *and* The Far Shore of Time*).*

The legendary science fiction writer now lives in the suburbs of Chicago with his wife, Professor Elizabeth Anne Hull.

You just turned ninety. How does that feel?

Well, I never planned on being ninety and don't know exactly how it happened ... but I guess it's better than the alternative.

Do you still stick with the four-pages-a-day regimen?

Yes and no. A couple of years ago, I began having serious breathing problems and decided to quit smoking. This has helped my breathing, but ruined my writing at least temporarily: Sixty years of writing with a cigarette burning in an ashtray beside me so fixed my physical behavior that I found it almost impossible to get any writing done. Over recent months, the situation has at least begun to improve, and I think I am back on track again.

There are rumors that you are working on another *Gateway* book. Is this true?

Yes, I'm working on another Heechee book. A couple of years ago, Bob Silverberg, who is very persuasive when he wants to be, coaxed me to write a Heechee novelette for an anthology he was editing. My wife and I were cruising in the eastern Mediterranean, and I wrote a story on the ship. It turned out to be too long for his book, so I wrote another and sent it to him. Then I realized I had about 30,000 words worth of Heechee stories, and resolved to write some more and make them into a book. It will be called *From Gateway to the Core* ... provided I finish writing it. [Author's note: The book was published in 2004 as *The Boy Who Lived Forever*.]

***Gateway* won the Hugo**, the Nebula and the John W. Campbell Memorial Award. It was also a bestseller, with over thirty printings. Did you expect such recognition when you wrote it?

I knew it was a good book. I didn't know that it would win all the awards, but I'm glad it did. I would have been disappointed if some other book had beaten it out. It's a good book. I've written a couple of sequels to it since, and I've published a lot of books. I'm not crazy about all of them. There are maybe twenty or thirty that I like; and of those, *Gateway* is maybe the one I like best or within the top couple anyhow. I change from day to day. I also like *Chernobyl* a lot and *The Years of the City*, but *Gateway*, I think, is about as good as I get.

***Gateway* is now a game.** Would you ever consider writing an interactive book?

I don't think I'll ever want to write an interactive book. It's more fun to write the novels and let someone else do the games.

You're a fan, writer and collector. At one time, you were a book and magazine editor, agent and even president of the Science Fiction Writers of America and of World Science Fiction, the international organization of people with professional connections to science fiction. Of all those roles, which ones did you enjoy the most?

Writer. All the others are work. There's a lot of pleasure to being editor under the right circumstances, but, it doesn't compare to being a writer.

In your lifetime, you've seen the invention of computers, rocket trips to the moon, VCRs, DVDs, cellular phones, all these scientific inventions and breakthroughs. Does science fiction sometimes get dwarfed by science fact?

No. All these came out of science fiction. None of them took me by surprise, because I had been reading about them for years before they happened. I was in Paris in August 1945, and I was getting a haircut in a barber shop off the Chantier, Lisse. And I was looking over the shoulder of the man next to me, and he had

Frederik Pohl (left) and author Michael McCarty at Pohl's office (photograph by Elizabeth Anne Hull, 1989).

a newspaper with a big headline, "Le Bomb et Amique." And the first thing I thought was that these crazy French will print anything in their papers. And then when I looked a little closer and realized it actually had happened. I felt, "Well, I knew it all along," and I had. Everybody who read science fiction knew that this was a good possibility. There are several kinds of science fiction that you can't write any more. You can't write about the first intelligent robot, the first trip to the moon or the first nuclear war, because they've happened, but the consequences of all these things are just getting clearer every day.

How do you still maintain an active fascination for science fiction?

What keeps me interested in science fiction is science. That is, the constantly unfolding observational and theoretical knowledge of how the universe works — and how this can be expressed in SF stories.

Are there trends in science fiction you don't care for?

I like all kinds of science fiction. What I don't care for is most combinations of SF and fantasy. To me they have nothing to say that C.L. Moore didn't say better long ago.

On the same topic, are there trends in science fiction that you think will become bigger?

The thing about SF is that isn't monolithic and doesn't have unique trends. It goes in all directions at once, as individual writers think of new things to explore and others learn from them.

What are your thoughts on rejection slips?

Rejection slips are the price we pay for wanting to be writers in the first place, I guess. Sort of a maturation rite, like circumcision or driver's ed.

In your work, you've often made such pointed comments on political and social matters.

I was always interested in society. I was a radical when I was a teenager, and I've been a Democrat ever since, which is basically a kind of radical compared to the Republicans. I've done a lot of reading on various political thinkers, all of the Utopians, and the kind of societies that I thought would be something to write about.

There's no doubt that there are things terribly wrong with our society. The hard part is trying to figure out how to make them better, which I haven't succeeded in doing. But one of the advantages of writing SF is that you can think about how other societies might work if the rules were a little different, and then write a story and see how people would be affected by that. Most of the science fiction I like best is like that although there's also quite a lot that's sort of a celebration of science and investigations into the unknown. But I do spend a lot of time writing what they call social science fiction and propose to go on doing so.

Satire is a predominant element in your work. Who were the satirists that you read?

The first fiction I ever remember reading was by Voltaire, his *Candide*. My mother gave it to me when I was about eight. She thought it was a fairy tale. Voltaire was one of the greatest satirists of the enlightenment. And I read Jonathan Swift and all the classic satirists.

There's an element of satire in most of the science fiction I liked best when I was beginning to read it. Even Edgar Rice Burroughs in his Mars books is really satirizing Earthly customs, religions and politics. Of course, *Brave New World*, Aldous Huxley's novel, was pure satire, and there were a couple of magazine writers (a man named Stanton A. Coblentz, in particular) who wrote a sort of heavy-handed, crude, but sometimes funny satirical science fiction. I guess they all influenced me, but then everything I read influences me.

Considering all the books you've read, the research you've done and the ideas you've pondered in your long career, what do you plan to study next?

I'm trying to master the essentials of quantum physics and cosmology. I've been trying to do that for at least twenty years, and I would not say that I am yet even close. The confounded scientists keep coming up with new stuff.

In your book *Narabedla Ltd.*, you wrote about the struggles of musicians. Did you ever want to be a musician?

I wanted to be a singer at one time. I would love to be a musician, but I never had any training in any instrument. I picked up a little bit of guitar and stuff like that. But I never really wanted to be anything more than I wanted to be a writer. But I would like also to have been a musician if I could.

Do you have a fondness for classical music?

Legendary science fiction author Frederik Pohl (photograph by Fred Fox Studio's Ltd., in the 1990s).

Mostly classical music. Mostly the romantic 18th century big orchestra music; and best of all, the violin concerto. It's somebody playing in front of a hundred musicians — sort of a contest between this one guy with the fiddle and all those other people. I like a lot of other music, too, unfortunately not rock and especially not country and western. I like a fair amount of pop music, operatic music — music in general. I usually have the radio going when I'm working, usually turned to a classical music station.

What are some of your favorite sci-fi films over the years?

I think the one I like best of all is *Things to Come*. It came out in 1936 and it just knocked me over. I think I saw it about twenty-five or thirty times. I also like *Forbidden Planet*. I'd been offered the chance to write a book version of the film before it came out and I didn't think it was going to be any good so I turned it down. Then when I saw it in the theater I kicked myself because it was really one of the very few science fiction movies with a story that could have been good in print.

The first science fiction movie I ever saw was called *Just Imagine*. It was released in 1930. It was about the incredible far future of 1980. In it, New York was all skyscrapers and people lived on pills. When a couple wanted a baby, they'd put a quarter into a machine and a baby came out. It was also Maureen O'Sullivan's first movie and I fell madly in love with her.

You knew some of the great SF writers. What is one of your fondest memories of Robert Heinlein?

Well, I have a lot. Most of them come from his writing, because the best part of any writer is what he writes, but I do remember spending time with him. I think the clearest single image of Bob Heinlein was in 1972, I believe it was, when he and I and a bunch of other SF writers were cruising on an American Lines Cruise Liner down to watch the launch of Apollo 17, the last manned Apollo flight to the moon. That was the only time I had ever seen one from offshore. There were a whole bunch of people on the ship; when they were ready to launch, we all got up on the deck, and we started looking toward the shore. We saw the sun rise in the East and go completely up across the sky, because the Apollo rocket launched. I turned around and looked over my shoulder, and I saw Bob Heinlein's face illuminated by the light of the rocket. Also there were Ted Sturgeon, Isaac Asimov and one or two others, and I wished I had my camera with me just to take a picture of these people in that light. But I didn't have a camera, so it's only in my head. But that's the time I remember. That's the picture I carry of Bob.

What's the hardest part of being a professional novelist?

Making yourself do it; assuming that you have acquired the fairly rudimentary skills necessary for putting what you think on paper. If you have something to say, the difficult part is making yourself sit down and say it. It is a very frustrating occupation, because you don't have anybody to tell you when you're through. If you have a job, you work from nine 'til five. At five o'clock, you go home. Even if you are an independent contractor, say a bricklayer; someone will say, "Lay a wall over there, so high and so long," and then you could tell when it's done.

With writing, you never know when it's done. You never know when it could stand a little more work somewhere. It's also kind of irritating to sit down at the word processor or typewriter and think, "I have 400 blank sheets of paper—I have to fill them somehow." If I thought in those terms, I would never get anything done. What I do is four pages a day, each day. Four pages I can manage.

You recently wrote *The Other End of Time*, *The Siege of Eternity* and *The Far Shore of Time*, which is part of Eschaton Sequence. What is Eschaton?

Eschaton is a theological term meaning when everything becomes all different, all the rules change. It has been used by physicist Frank Tippler to describe the time when the universe has expanded as far as it can, and then it collapses back into itself again in what they call the Big Crush. When it's all back in one piece again, that's what he calls the Eschaton.

What do you think the twenty-second century will be like?

We can't do that in a thirty-minute interview [*laughs*]. One of the local Chicago newspapers asked me to name five things which will no longer be around in the year 2210. I said, "There will not be any computers, television sets, traffic jams, hospitals or airports." That I'm pretty sure of. Whatever else happens depends a great deal on what people make happen.

There have been a lot of attempts by pretty bright and well-informed people to figure out methodologies for forecasting the future. They figured out a whole bunch of really snazzy ones: Delphi Herman Kahn scenario writing, methodological mapping, trendline extrapolations, etc. All had one thing in common. None of them worked. A man named Dennis Gabor, who is best known for inventing the hologram, is also one of the leaders in the future studies discipline. He summarized it all when he said, "It is impossible to predict the future. The best we can do is invent it."

You really can't say much about what will be in the twenty-second century. You can only say what can be and what may be, and there are certain things there won't be, like the five I mentioned.

On the same theme, what kind of "futuribles" intrigue you or concern you these days?

"Futuribles" that interest me right now: (a) seeing just how bad the weather is going to get with the global warming [author's note: to find out more about this, read Pohl and Isaac Asimov's *Our Angry Earth*], (b) trying to imagine what the world will be like when computers are tinier than a button, cheaper than a jelly bean and in absolutely everything we own, and (c) anticipating the results of the coming stock market megacrash.

You've written some very sexy science fiction. What is the secret of writing sexual passages in speculative fiction?

The secret is to write them only when the story is incomplete without them. This is also the secret of writing any other kind of passage.

I think your new book *O Pioneer!* is one of your best to date.

Thanks for the kind word. It's been getting some nice reviews, too. It's the first book I've written just for the fun of it, so I couldn't have been more pleased. Now if only some of the Nebula and Hugo voters happen feel the same way [*laughs*].

What was the inspiration behind *Man Plus*?

The inspiration did not come from me, but from a woman who wanted to produce a film. She had the idea that the movie should be about cyborgs in space. That's all she had to say about it. I spent a couple of months trying to write a screenplay, just a treatment for her. It went nowhere. I never got paid for it either [*laughs*]. After I put all this work into it, I decided to make a novel out of it.

What are your thoughts on the sequel you wrote with Thomas T. Thomas, *Mars Plus*?

The sequel came about because Jim Baen, the publisher of Baen Books, took me to lunch one day, got me loaded and said, "I want you to write an outline for a sequel and have someone else write the book," and I agreed. I haven't done that very often and I'm not sure I want to do it again. Actually, I thought Thomas T. Thomas did a very good job of writing, not the book that I would have written, but a satisfying book based on my ideas. I would have written it differently, but he did things I wouldn't have thought to do. He had some very nice touches in it.

Venus has been the setting for several of your novels. Does the planet have any special appeal for you?

Venus is closest to the Earth in most respects. The only ways in which it's different are the temperature and the air pressure. And that, apparently, is because it's about 40 million miles closer to the sun. So, if you could deal with the temperature, which is hot enough to melt lead, or the air pressure, which is enough to crush any normal living thing, it would be a good planet to live on. I guess I've also written about every planet in the solar system that I thought could possibly support anybody walking on its surface. The big ones — Jupiter, Saturn, Uranus, Neptune — don't seem to have any surfaces so they don't count, but you can put stories on Mars, Venus, Mercury, Pluto, the moon, Callisto, Ganymede and various other satellites. But Venus, I think, is logical; it's an easy place to get to from here. It's the closest planet. Most of the time it's even closer than Mars. I have no special other fondness for it.

In *The Way the Future Was*, you wrote about authors coming to your house, and there were certain clubs that you guys would meet at, and you got a sense of community among the science fiction writers. Do you still feel that community today?

Oh, yeah, still. Sure. There are a lot more of us now than there used to be. In Science Fiction of America. I think there are 750 members or something like that. They aren't really all science fiction writers. Some of them don't write science fiction at all. They write fantasy, which is kindred but not quite the same, and some of the others have only written a little bit. There're still a lot of science fiction writers, and there are probably about a thousand more scattered around the rest of the world. A larger number in Japan and the Soviet Union, quite a few in England and quite a few in Western Europe, and others all over. When I was an editor, I got a manuscript from a man who said he was the second best science fiction writer in Iran, which indicates there are at least two. I never heard of him or the other one either, but they're there.

I know quite a few writers and so on from all over the world, because I run into them all at various foreign meetings, or sometimes they come to America. We had a friend from the Soviet Union visiting here last month. We've had friends from France, England, China and all sorts of places.

You hear about science fiction during the Golden Age. But what was sci-fi like during the McCarthy-blacklist era?

In the United States in the 1950s during the McCarthy period I used to know a minister in Los Angeles who sold *Galaxy* and *Astounding* and a couple of other magazines in his vestry after the services because he said they were the only free speech left in America. It was not untrue. It wasn't wholly true, but there was some truth to it.

In *The Day the Martians Came*, humans make jokes about the aliens. Do you feel that humans would be chauvinistic about aliens who aren't like us?

Well, it has never been tested out because we haven't found any aliens to be chauvinistic to, but I think people tend to somewhat fear and resent any possible competition. You see that in all the ethnic arguments going on all over the world, and the fact that people tell ethnic jokes. It's a way of expressing hostility, which is also a way of expressing fear: These people aren't quite like me, and I don't know what they're going to be doing. And I think that would be even more so if you found intelligent aliens. The point of the story *The Day the Martians Came* is that maybe if we found some intelligent aliens, people could transfer all their hostilities to them, and then we wouldn't have to spend so much time hating each other. Whether this is likely to happen or not, I don't know, but I thought it was pretty interesting to think so.

You co-wrote *Our Angry Earth* with Isaac Asimov. Weren't you responsible for the publication of Asimov's first book, *Pebble in the Sky*.

I was his agent for a while when I was a literary agent in the 1950s. He had already written a textbook on biochemistry with two other people. Each had written one-third of it. But the first book published on his own [*Pebble*]—yes, I placed that for him.

Can you give us an Isaac Asimov anecdote?

Oh—I have about a million of them. We were both teenagers and lived in Brooklyn. He lived at one end of Prospect Park and I lived at the other end and when I was desperate for a malted milk I would walk across the park and his mother would make one for me. She was my major source for free malted milks.

Anything else you would like to add?
 I'm just back from a Panama Canal cruise, on which I did a lot of writing. Cruises are turning out to be about my best writing venue — the phone doesn't ring. The Canal trip was special. I spent the first year of my life in The Zone, in the town of Gatun, where my father had a job working on the locks, and had never been back since. So I did want to see the place and I loved the trip.

Books by Frederik Pohl

SPACE MERCHANTS

The Space Merchants (1952) (with C.M. Kornbluth)
The Merchant's War (1984)
Venus, Inc. (1984) (with C.M. Kornbluth)

UNDERSEA EDEN (WITH JACK WILLIAMSON)

Undersea Quest (1954)
Undersea Fleet (1955)
Undersea City (1958)
The Undersea Trilogy (1992)

STARCHILD (WITH JACK WILLIAMSON)

The Reefs of Space (1964)
Starchild (1965)
Rogue Star (1969)
The Starchild Trilogy (1980)

SAGA OF CUCKOO (WITH JACK WILLIAMSON)

Farthest Star (1975)
Wall Around a Star (1975)
The Saga of Cuckoo (1983)

HEECHEE

Gateway (1976)
Beyond the Blue Event Horizon (1980)
Heechee Rendezvous (1984)
The Annals of the Heechee (1987)

The Gateway Trip: Tales and Vignettes of the Heechee (1990)
The Boy Who Would Live Forever: A Novel of Gateway (2004)

Eschaton

The Other End of Time (1996)
The Siege of Eternity (1997)
The Far Shore of Time (1999)
The Eschaton Sequence (1999)

Novels

Search the Sky (1954) (with C.M. Kornbluth)
Gladiator-at-Law (1955) (with C.M. Kornbluth)
Preferred Risk (1955) (writing as Edson McCann)
Presidential Year (1956) (with C.M. Kornbluth)
Slave Ship (1956)
Wolfbane (1957) (with C.M. Kornbluth)
Drunkard's Walk (1960)
A Plague of Pythons (1964)
The Age of the Pussyfoot (1965)
Man Plus (1976)
Jem (1979)
Syzygy (1981)
The Cool War (1981)
Starburst (1982)
The Years of the City (1984)
Black Star Rising (1985)
Terror (1986)
The Coming of the Quantum Cats (1986)
Chernobyl (1987)
The Day the Martians Came (1988)
Land's End (1988) (with Jack Williamson)
Narabedla, Ltd. (1988)
Homegoing (1989)
The World at the End of Time (1990)
Outnumbering the Dead (1990)
The Singers of Time (1991) (with Jack Williamson)
Stopping at Slowyear (1991)
Mining the Oort (1992)
Mars Plus (1994) (with Thomas T. Thomas)
The Voices of Heaven (1994)
O Pioneer! (1998)
The Last Theorem (2008) (with Arthur C. Clarke)

Collections

Alternating Currents (1956)
The Case Against Tomorrow (1957)

Tomorrow Times Seven (1959)
The Man Who Ate the World (1960)
Turn Left at Thursday (1961)
The Wonder Effect (1962) (with C.M. Kornbluth)
The Abominable Earthman (1963)
Digits and Dastards (1966)
Day Million (1970)
Gold at the Starbow's End (1972)
The Best of Frederik Pohl (1975)
The Early Pohl (1976)
In the Problem Pit: And Other Stories (1976)
Critical Mass (1977) (with C.M. Kornbluth)
Survival Kit (1979)
Before the Universe (1980) (with C.M. Kornbluth)
Planets Three (1981)
Midas World (1983)
Pohlstars (1984)
Tales from the Planet Earth: A Novel with Nineteen Authors (1986)
Bipohl (1987)
Our Best: The Best of Frederik Pohl and C.M. Kornbluth (1987) *(with C.M. Kornbluth)*
The Future Quartet: Earth in the Year 2042 (1994) *(with Ben Bova, Jerry Pournelle and Charles Sheffield)*
Platinum Pohl (2001)

ANTHOLOGIES EDITED

Beyond the End of Time (1952)
Tomorrow, the Stars (1952) Edited by Robert A. Heinlein (edited by Pohl)
Shadow of Tomorrow (1953)
Star Science Fiction Stories No. 2 (1953)
Star Science Fiction Stories No. 1 (1953)
Assignment in Tomorrow (1954)
Star Science Fiction Stories No. 3 (1954)
Star Science Fiction Stories No. 4 (1958)
Star Science Fiction Stories No. 5 (1959)
Star Science Fiction Stories No. 6 (1959)
The Expert Dreamers (1962)
Star Short Novels (1963)
The Eleventh Galaxy Reader (1964)
The Eighth Galaxy Reader (1965)
Worlds of If 116 (1967)
Star Fourteen (1968)
Worlds of If 128 (1968)
Worlds of If 129 (1969)
Nightmare Age (1970)
Best Science Fiction for 1972 (1972)
Jupiter (1973) (with Carol Pohl)
Science Fiction: The Great Years (1973) (with Carol Pohl)
Science Fiction—The Great Years: Volume Two (1974) (with Carol Pohl)

The Science Fiction Roll of Honor (1975)
Science Fiction Discoveries (1976) (with Carol Pohl)
Science Fiction of the 40s (1978) (with Damon Knight)
Galaxy: Thirty Years of Innovative Science Fiction (1979)
Great Science Fiction Series: Stories from the Best of the Science Fiction Series from 1944 to 1980 by All-Time Favorite Writers (1980)
Galaxy 2 (1981)
Yesterday's Tomorrows: Favorite Stories from Forty Years as a Science Fiction Editor (1982)
Worlds of If: A Retrospective Anthology (1986) (with Martin H Greenberg, Joseph Olander)
The SFWA Grand Masters, Volume 3 (1992)
The SFWA Grand Masters, Volume 2 (1996)
The SFWA Grand Masters (1999)

Nonfiction

Practical Politics (1971)
The Viking Settlements of North America (1972)
The Way the Future Was: A Memoir (1978)
Science Fiction Studies in Film (1980)
New Visions: A Collection of Modern Science Fiction Art (1982)
Our Angry Earth (1991) (with Isaac Asimov)
Prince Henry Sinclair: His Expedition to the New World in 1398 (1995)
Chasing Science: Science as Spectator Sport (1995)

Awards

Pohl has won most of the awards the science-fiction field has to offer, including the Edward E. Smith and Donald A. Wollheim memorial awards, the International John W. Campbell award (twice), the French Prix Apollo, the Yugoslavian Vizija, the Nebula (three times, including the "Grand Master" Nebula for lifetime contributions to the field) and the Hugo (six times; he is the only person ever to have won the Hugo both as writer and as editor). Awards from sources outside the science-fiction community include the American Book Award, the annual award of the Popular Culture Association, and the United Nations Society of Writers Award. Other honors include election as a fellow to both the British Interplanetary Society and the American Association for the Advancement of Science.

> "Quentin Tarantino and I had the same manager for years and then he got big."
>
> — *Linnea Quigley*

Queen of the Scream Queens: Linnea Quigley

Linnea Quigley is one of the horror industry's most beloved scream queens. She has made close to one hundred movies, has appeared in Fangoria *magazine a number of times and is still a big draw at horror conventions across the country. She was ranked number nine on* Maxim *magazine's "Hottest Women of Horror Movies."*

Quigley's list of horror cult classics includes Return of the Living Dead, Night of the Demons, Hollywood Chainsaw Hookers, Sorority Babes in the Slimeball Bowl-O-Rama, Burial of the Rats, Silent Night, Deadly Night *(I have a warm spot for her "Best Impaled-on-Antlers Performance" in that film),* Nightmare Sisters *and* Jack-O. *She also produces movies and plays guitar and sings in an all-girl rock band, The Skirts. She was the first woman inducted into the Horror Hall of Fame by* Fangoria. *This from a lady whose first big break in showbiz was acting in a toothpaste commercial.*

Quigley decided to move to Florida to be closer to her parents in the early 2000s. She currently lives in South Florida with her myriad pets and is a big supporter of animal rights. Currently, she is planning on moving back to California. She is queen of the Bs — long live the queen! Her websites are: www.linneaquigley.net, www.myspace.com/originaltrash and www.linneaquigleycircle.com.

How did you go from living in Davenport, Iowa, to becoming a Hollywood successful scream queen?

Anybody who goes to L.A. gets sucked into the acting trap and then it's like, you're working at some lousy job or something and everybody goes, "Oh, you should be an actress or a model, you're very glamorous." You're more attainable than in Iowa, so I went for it! I started getting modeling gigs and I took acting classes and even though I was real shy I ended up doing okay and I was totally shocked that it actually all happened.

Scream queen Linnea Quigley during the 1980s (courtesy Linnea Quigley).

You made close to a hundred films — that is amazing for someone who "accidentally fell into acting." At which point did you decide you enjoyed it and wanted to pursue a career in the movies?

I never thought there would be a way for me, it seemed like it was so unattainable. I was born in Iowa. I didn't think I was pretty enough, I was shy. I didn't think I would be able to utter any words or do anything. I wished and wished — it took a lot of conquering my fears, [because] this business is pretty rough on people. In the beginning, it was scary. I started out doing extra work, one-liners and things like that and learned all about the business. I would help out on different things and learn as much as I could.

Was there an early movie when you saw yourself on the screen and said, "I'm a professional actress now — I finally made it"?

Did you read my old diaries [*laughs*]? One of the first movies that I spoke in, *Fairy Tales*, I remember writing down in my diary: "Oh my God, I am a star now. I'm in a movie, I went to a theater to see it." It wasn't much of a part. To me, "This is it."

In *Return of the Living Dead*, when you became a zombie, the makeup effect they used on you, looks like it was a mask with an open mouth. Did you have a hard time biting people when you probably couldn't move your mouth?

It was horrible. There were two masks made. Director Dan O'Bannon had Kenny Myers make them. For the close-up, the mask was way down.

They had it when I was going to bite the people, the "Send more cops" scenes and such. They used the mask for the close-ups. He wanted the mask really exaggerated.

In *Return of the Living Dead*, you stripped on top of a crypt that was lit by burning torches and was covered in sawdust that was supposed to be Spanish moss. Were you worried about something catching fire?

No. But I was getting very dizzy because the torches were those sulfuric acid torches they use when there is an accident [road flares]. The fumes were going right up into my face. We did take after take and they lit them and those fumes were brutal.

In the last half of the movie, you portrayed a naked zombie in the rain. Was that uncomfortable?

Yes. It was very cold out. L.A. gets cold at night, the temperature drops like crazy. I was freezing. I couldn't sit down because the makeup would rub off. I couldn't put a towel around me because the makeup would rub off. It was just horrible.

What was it like working on *Night of the Demons*?

I kept telling them I won't go up for the role because the cast was all teenagers and I was sick of going to the interviews and they wanted someone who was twelve [*laughs*]. It was weird because everyone was eighteen. I didn't know how to say some of the words in the script, like "wuss"; I kept saying "wus."

Were you about 25 then?

Yeah. There was a huge age gap between us.

Talk about the remake of *Night of the Demons*.

It is many years later and everybody is wearing less clothing [*laughs*] — oh no, that doesn't happen [*laughs*]. It is a little creepier; there was a lot more money to work with. The writers, the director, everybody is great. Kevin Tenney [director of the original] approved it — that is a good thing because most people wouldn't want a remake to be out there and be awful. I think people will be happy with the remake. I always hate it when people go, "They shouldn't have done a remake."*

---

*According to Quigley's manager, Danna Taylor, "There were a lot of people who found out about the remake. They were really irritated, and said, 'We are not going to see it because Linnea is not in it.' We couldn't announce that Linnea *was* in it, until the production company announced it. When production announced it, hundreds of e-mails came in, saying, 'We approve of this now because Linnea is actually in it.'"

What else are you working on now?
Post Mortem America, 2021— that is going to be real kick-ass. That should be put out very soon. There are a bunch of other ones which are in production. I am doing a lot of writing and producing. I co-produced *Vampire Theater*, which is coming out on DVD. *The Notorious Colonel Steel* just came out and *Savage Streets* was re-released as a special edition and so was *Hollywood Chainsaw Hookers*. I also did a scream track for a song called "scream queen" by a band called Rip Snorter. It is going to rock!

What's your secret for continuing to look so good? Do your zombie workouts have anything to do with that?
Yes [*laughs*]. I must say, living in California though is the best treatment for anyone — I should be moving back here soon. That is one of the best workouts.

What is your opinion of computer generated images in genre films?
I don't like them. I remember watching *Terminator 2* and that was the first time I really ever saw CGI effects. It was like, "Ugh!" It just wrecks the movie for me.

Are there any films you regret making?
No, because it got me where I was going. Sometimes now, I look back at mainly how I was treated, and I think, Danna Taylor who is my manager — she is amazing, she does things right. Everybody else just kind of sent me out to the wolves — they didn't care what I'd be doing or if I'd be cold or the food I'd eat or anything. The others were so artificial type of people. Back to the question, I regret that I worked on films where they were not treating me or paying me right.

Any projects you regret not making?
Not really. There were films I could have done, but couldn't due to circumstances.

Which films are you the most proud of?
Of course, *Return of the Living Dead*— the way it came out and everything. *Night of the Demons*, both the original and remake, I am excited, plus it's really weird seeing another actress [Bobbi Sue Luther] playing Suzanne; that is going to be weird. It makes you realize how much things have evolved and how long I have been in the film business — whoa — scary [*laughs*]. I liked doing *Hollywood Chainsaw Hookers*. *Hoodoo for Voodoo* was fun. *Treasure of the Moon Goddess* was a blast. *Savage Streets* for me was a hard part. Everybody says, "You didn't have any lines"— it was really hard to do, it was a challenge, not being able to make any kind of noise.

This one I am doing with Cameron Scott, *Post Mortem America, 2021*—it is a really great part. The weird thing is, I met him when he was sixteen. A lot of years later, he always wanted to make a movie and he did it. That is amazing.

Do you have copies of all of them?

No, some I don't, I need to find them. A lot of them are hard to find. A lot of them are, "That was a great performance," but I haven't even seen it. I am not sure if it is released or how to get hold of it.

Some of those 80 movies that came out on video aren't available on DVD or Blu-Ray.

I know it. Those movies like *Sorority Babes in the Slimeball Bowl-A-Rama*—I liked too, it was fun. We shot it in San Marcos, in an all-night bowling alley. The crew was like family, it was a blast. It is so different now. It isn't like a family any more, because there are so many production companies.

You helped to produce *Creepozoids, Dead End, The Girl I Want, Linnea Quigley's Horror Workout* and *Murder Weapon*. How did that come about?

I was working a lot with David DeCoteau [director of *Sorority Babes in the Slimeball Bowl-A-Rama* and *Creepozoids*] and he asked me to co-produce and I said, "Yeah." I jumped on it because I always wanted to do something besides acting.

If you had an unlimited budget, what kind of film would you produce?

Cynthia Garris and I have written a screenplay, kind of the old scary-movie type about saving animals in a lab. It was pretty dark, a lot of action, things like that going on. It was a good script, as I remember. We tried at the time to go to a few places—it was really hard at that time, they were doing movies mostly for two million or down to sixty thousand. I still have the synopsis and everything.

You wrote the books *Bio & Chainsaws, I'm Screaming as Fast as I Can, Skin* and, of course, our collaboration, the short story "Wizard of Ooze." What else are you working on in the literary and screenwriting departments?

With Danna Taylor, I'm working on a bunch of writing assignments right after the craziness of the holidays and everything. Danna is a great writer.

You also had a part in *Nightmare on Elm Street 4: The Dream Master*.

I played the soul coming out of Freddy's chest. The stunt went wrong, the huge Freddy statue fell. We almost got killed. The one lady working the head, the puppeteer (Mecki Heussen) fell onto concrete, she was probably about three stories up.

158 • *Masters of Imagination*

Have you ever appeared in *Playboy* magazine?

Three times: The "Girls of Rock N Roll," a dancing one and "B-Movie Queens" pictorials.

How long did it take for the makeup artists to apply body paint in *Hollywood Chainsaw Hookers*?

Eleven hours with three people. They thought it would only take three hours and then they had to keep calling in people. I even called my ex-husband [special effects wizard Steve Johnson]. It was ridiculous. It was a very long day.

Did you like the way the effect came out on the film?

Oh, yeah. The effect was great but standing there for that long was horrible. I get very fidgety.

What was it like working with low-budget writer-director Fred Olen Ray on *Hollywood Chainsaw Hookers*?

Interesting. He's got a very sarcastic way of doing things. He keeps things moving along. He knows what he's doing. He was fun.

You've done a number of films with scream queen Michelle Bauer. What's she like on- and off-screen?

She is great, she is amazing. It is so much fun working with her because she is so down-to-earth. She is never, "I am a star." She is just a happy, go-watch-football and hang-out-type person.

Have chainsaw will travel — Linnea Quigley from *Hollywood Chainsaw Hookers* (Camp Video, 1988) (courtesy Fred Olen Ray).

How did you get involved with animal rights?

I got involved after watching this news documentary when I was twenty-one years old. The show was about the experiments they do on animals. Those images burned into my brain. I had to help out after that.

Why do you think guys are attracted to scream queens so much?

I don't know. Some of the conventions girls call themselves scream queens but they haven't done any (what I'd consider) scream queen movies. It has changed a lot, but there haven't been a whole lot of new scream queens lately.

What is your take on the current popularity of extreme horror films like *Hostel* and the *Saw* movies?

I think it is going back to *Last House on the Left* and [movies] like that. Where movies were really bloody and realistic. They are concentrating a lot on torturing women. It is the monster next door opposed to the monster from beyond.

Is there any role you wouldn't take?

[Danna and I] turn them down on a daily basis. I look at the scripts and go, "Oh my God." We hear so-and-so is going to do that movie and it was offered to us because they had read it. The script is really bad.

Any unfulfilled fantasy about working with big-name stars or directors?

Yeah, Rob Zombie. Quentin Tarantino. Quentin and I had the same manager for years and then he got big. The lady who manages him, Cathryn James—*she* got him there. Robert Rodriguez [director of *From Dusk Till Dawn* and *Planet Terror*] would be great to work with. I'd like to work with Mick Garris again. I've known Mick and Cynthia Garris for so long. He's a great guy.

Cheech and Chong are making a comeback and you appeared in two of their films, *Nice Dreams* and *Still Smokin'*. Are they as wild and crazy as in their movies?

Cheech is really a nice, smart guy. Cheech is really into his career, a happy guy, a genuine person. It is so cool that he broke that barrier and got onto *Nash Bridges*. Tommy Chong, I don't know that well; he is more quiet.

Any advice to ladies looking to break into the horror film field?

You've got to trust your gut feeling. There are a lot of people I've helped and given advice to, but they don't follow it. You get tired of repeating yourself again and again.

And get everything in writing. Get to the bank with them, maybe bring a taser if you have to. Turn into the psycho that you are playing [*laughs*].

Last words?

I want people not to be so hard on themselves if they are in this business. There will be people who will try to take you down because *they* are going down. You've just got to be careful of that. You can get very upset about it. You've just got to keep your confidence and be around people who are positive and good.

Linnea Quigley Filmography

Psycho from Texas (1975)
Auditions (1978)
Adult Fairytales (1978)
Deathsport (1978) (uncredited)
Summer Camp (1979)
Don't go Near the Park (1981)
Cheech & Chong's Nice Dreams (1981)
Graduation Day (1981)
Young Warriors (1983)
Get Crazy (1983) (uncredited)
Cheech & Chong's: Still Smokin (1983) (uncredited) ... Blonde in Spa
Nudes in Limbo (1983) (uncredited) ... Model
Kidnapped Girls Agency (1983)
Silent Night, Deadly Night (1984)
The Black Room (1984)
Party Games for Adults Only (1984)
Fatal Games (1984)
The Return of the Living Dead (1985)
Beverly Hills Girls (1986)
Avenged (1986)
Sweethearts (1986)
Scorpion (1986)
Creepozoids (1987)
Nightmare Sisters (1987)
Treasure of the Moon Goddess (1987)
A Nightmare on Elm Street 4: The Dream Master (1988) (Soul from Freddy's Chest)
Dead Heat (1988) (uncredited)
Hollywood Chainsaw Hookers (1988)
Sorority Babes in the Slimeball Bowl-O-Rama (1988)
Night of the Demons (1988)
Robot Ninja (1989)
Witchtrap (1989)
Vice Academy (1989)
Blood Nasty (1989)
Dr. Alien (1989)
American Rampage (1989)
Assault of the Party Nerds (1989)
Sexbomb (1989)
Deadly Embrace (1989)
Murder Weapon (1989)
Vice Academy Part 2 (1990)
Diggin' Up Business (1990)
Guyver (1991)
Virgin High (1991)
Innocent Blood (1992)
Blood Church (1992)
Beach Babes from Beyond (1993)

The Girl I Want (1993)
Pumpkinhead II: Blood Wings (1994)
Vampire Hunter (1994)
Jack-O (1995) *Stripteaser* (1995) (uncredited) *Assault of the Party Nerds 2: The Heavy Petting Detective* (1995)
Burial of the Rats (1995)
Fatal Frames (1996)
Sick-O-Pathics (1996)
Hollywood Cops (1997)
Boogie Boy (1998) *Moving Targets* (1998) *Death Mask* (1998) *Curse of the Lesbian Love Goddess* (1998)
Mari-Cookie and the Killer Tarantula in 8 Legs to Love You (1998)
Play It to the Bone (1999) (uncredited)
Kolobos (1999)
Animals (1999)
The Killer Eye (1999) (uncredited)
Blind Target (2000)
Sex Files: Pleasureville (2000)
The Monster Man (2001)
Horrorvision (2001) (uncredited)
Kannibal (2001)
Venice Beach (2001)
Scream Queen (2002)
Zombiegeddon (2003)
Charlie and Sadie (2003)
Corpses Are Forever (2003)
Super Hero Central (2004)
The Rockville Slayer (2004)
Frost (2004)
Whispers from a Shallow Grave (2006)
Hoodoo for Voodoo (2006)
Voices from the Graves (2006)
Pretty (2007)
Each Time I Kill (2007)
A Drive with Linnea and Donald (2008)
The Notorious Colonel Steel (2008)
Spring Break Massacre (2008)
Night of the Demons (2009)
It Came from Trafalgar (2009)
RiffRaff (2009)
Vampitheatre (2009)
Night on Has-Been Mountain (2009)
La femme vampir (2009)
Strangers Online (2009)
Post Mortem, America 2021 (2010)

Books by Linnea Quigley

Bio & Chainsaw (1991)
I'm Screaming as Fast as I Can (1995)
Skin (1999)
Midnight Premiere (anthology) edited by Tom Piccirilli (Cemetery Dance Books)
Short story: "The Wizard of Ooze" by Linnea Quigley and Michael McCarty (2007)
Little Creatures (short story collection) by Michael McCarty (Sam's Dot Publishing)

Awards

Linnea Quigley was the first woman inducted into the Horror Hall of Fame by *Fangoria* magazine.

"Ed Wood was a very gregarious, outgoing guy. He was very excited that anyone remembered him or would want to hire him to write. It's a real shame he didn't live long enough to enjoy the fame he would later receive."

— Fred Olen Ray

One-Man Movie Industry: Fred Olen Ray
by Mark McLaughlin and Michael McCarty

The movie titles instantly grab your attention: Attack of the 60-Foot Centerfold, Scream Queen Hot Tub Party, Dinosaur Girls, The Brain Leeches, Beverly Hills Vamp, Bad Girls from Mars, Invisible Mom, Hollywood Chainsaw Hookers *and more. You know these movies haven't won any Oscars, but even so, they have their place in the hearts of their fans. These are cult classics — campy, vampy and beloved by adventurous movie watchers everywhere.*

Those titles and more are the brainchildren of Fred Olen Ray. Over the past 30-plus years, this prolific producer, director, and screenwriter has made more than 100 films, and is showing no signs of slowing down.

Fred was born in Ohio in 1954 and grew up in Florida, where he worked with film legend Buster Crabbe on the movie Alien Dead. *He later moved to Southern California so he could be closer to the beating heart of America's film industry. He has worked in the genres of horror, science fiction, action-adventure, crime dramas, soft-core erotic films and also some family films. Over the years, he has used a variety of pseudonyms, including Bill Carson, S. Carver, Roger Collins, Peter Daniels, Nick Medina, Nicholas Medina, Sam Newfield, Ed Raymond, Sherman Scott, and Peter Stewart. He has even tried his hand at professional wrestling under the name of Fabulous Freddie Valentine.*

His early movies — often low on budget but high on energy — appeared at drive-in theaters and grindhouses venues. More current movies have been released straight to DVD and/or to Cinemax, HBO and Showtime. Many of his films are released by his own DVD company, Retromedia.

What inspired you to follow a career in films?

Like a lot of kids, I was influenced by *Famous Monsters of Filmland* magazine and their articles about how other kids were making their own movies using their parents' 8mm cameras. I grew up mostly in Florida in a middle-class family.

What was the first movie you remember seeing?

My earliest memories are *The Alamo* and *Master of the World*, about 1960, I'd imagine.

Joking and smoking, director Fred Olen Ray (photograph by Dan Golden, 2000).

How did you get into the movie industry?

I started out in television and radio in Orlando, Florida, and made some very bad low-budget features on the weekends while working at the station. I eventually got stale at the station and decided to give California a shot.

One of your early movies, *Alien Dead*, was made for $12,000, of which $2,000 went to guest star Buster Crabbe. How did you get him to come out of retirement for only two grand?

I was a cameraman for *The Golden Age Olympics*, which Buster Crabbe was the grand marshal of, and I approached him there. He had friends in the Orlando area so he was keen to come back on someone else's dime ... and I do mean dime!

In *Alien Dead* **there is the line,** "She's deader than Mother's Day in an orphanage." Did you write that or was that Martin Allen Nicholas?

That was actually a gag tossed in by the actor Dennis Underwood, who was a funny guy.

You met Edward D. Wood Jr. What was he like?

Ed Wood was a very gregarious, outgoing guy. He was very excited that anyone remembered him or would want to hire him to write. It's a real shame he didn't live long enough to enjoy the fame he would later receive.

Why was *Hollywood Chainsaw Hookers* called *Hollywood Hookers* in England? Did they object to chainsaws more than hookers?

The UK had a thing about the word "chainsaw," they forbid it. I used to say they were all down with hookers because that's what they had the most of ... but I was just kidding, of course.

In 2008, you released a 20th anniversary edition of *Hollywood Chainsaw Hookers*. Why do you think the film has held up?

I think it's an honest exploitation film. Definitely a product of its time with a certain awareness of what came before it.

Hollywood Chainsaw Hookers and some of your other movies were featured in *Playboy* during the '80s. How did it feel to have your films featured next to Playboy bunnies?

Any PR is good PR... better than being hyped in *Nugget*. *Playboy* was the top of the line.

Should directors have the previous experience of being an actor?

Probably not.... Actors can be very funky people. I've always likened running a set to running a day care center. Directing and acting are two *very* different jobs.

Do you think the old black-and-white horror films will be lost to future generations raised on CGI effects? It's sad to think of Lugosi's Dracula, for example, fading into obscurity.

I know my kids have always steered clear of anything not in color, but I'm sure a resurgence will happen, like it did with Bogart and Dean. The old films will continue to entertain a certain group.

Who was the most memorable star you've ever featured — meaning, one who made the experience of working with them, for whatever reason, impossible to forget?

For good, bad and ho-hum I would say Lee Van Cleef, Telly Savalas, John Carradine, Cliff Robertson, Morgan Fairchild, Udo Kier, Tom Berenger and maybe Tanya Roberts.

Does the casting couch still exist in Hollywood today?

I couldn't tell you. I've never seen such a thing, but I do know that some directors try to find their next date amongst cast members. I'm not naming names.

What are the major challenges for indie filmmakers?

Getting the money raised, and getting the money back, are the toughest things. There is no good market right now for small films. Almost everyone is losing their shirt.

Which of your movies would you consider to be your best?
The Shooter.

Are vampire movies the cheapest of all horror films to make (with the possible exception of "invisible man" movies)?
Invisibility films are actually tough, because there are so many effects shots in them. I'd say vampires are even cheaper than zombies, but zombies come close.

You've made some movies with some pretty wild monsters in them. Which one was your favorite?
Probably the creature in *Deep Space*. It was big and rolled around on a track. I wish that would come out on DVD!

If you could remake any classic movie, no expense spared, which one would it be?
I'm not a fan of remaking classic films. I wouldn't mind making *Halloween 8*, but I wouldn't want to tackle a remake of John Carpenter's original…

You've worked with a number of scream queens over the years. Who do you think were the sexiest?
My vote always goes to Michelle Bauer for sexiest and funniest. Not too much complaining. I'm a pretty even-tempered guy and never push people very hard during the shoot. I like to hit it and quit it.

What's on the horizon?
We're still running Retromedia DVD and I'm still directing and producing at a higher level than ever. I might be the luckiest guy working today. Last year I made four features and produced a mini-series in Hawaii!

People always ask me what I'd really like to be doing and I tell them in all honesty I have everything I want in life. I have a beautiful loving wife, great children, a dog, a big house and a nice car…. Short of winning the lottery that just about covers it for me.

The Movies and TV Programs of Fred Olen Ray

DIRECTOR

Honey Britches (1971), a.k.a. *Death Farm; Demented Death Farm Massacre: The Movie; Hillbilly Hooker; Moonshiners' Women*

The Brain Leeches (1977)
Alien Dead (1980), a.k.a. *It Fell from the Sky; Swamp of the Blood Leeches; The Alien Dead*
Scalps (1983)
Biohazard (1985)
Armed Response (1986), a.k.a. *Jade Jungle*
The Tomb (1986)
The Phantom Empire (1986)
Commando Squad (1987)
Cyclone (1987)
Deep Space (1987)
Evil Spawn (1987), a.k.a. *Alien Within; Alive by Night; Deadly Sting; Metamorphosis*
Hollywood Chainsaw Hookers (1988), a.k.a. *Hollywood Hookers*
Prison Ship (1988), a.k.a. *Adventures of Taura; Prison Ship Star Slammer; Star Slammer; Starslammer; Starslammer: The Escape*
Beverly Hills Vamp (1988)
Warlords (1989)
Terminal Force (1989)
Alienator (1989)
Mob Boss (1990)
Demon Cop (1990)
Bad Girls from Mars (1991)
Haunting Fear (1991)
Spirits (1991)
Inner Sanctum (1991)
Scream Queen Hot Tub Party (1991) (as Bill Carson), a.k.a. *Hollywood Scream Queen Hot Tub Party*
Wizards of the Demon Sword (1991)
Evil Toons (1992)
Dinosaur Girls (1993)
Witch Academy (1993), a.k.a. *Little Devils*
Inner Sanctum II (1994), a.k.a. *Inner Sanctum 2*
Possessed by the Night (1994)
Dinosaur Island (1994)
Mind Twister (1994)
Droid Gunner (1995), a.k.a. *Phoenix 2*
Bikini Drive-In (1995)
Attack of the 60-Foot Centerfold (1995)
Star Hunter (1995) (as Sam Newfield)
Friend of the Family II (1996) (as Nicholas Medina), a.k.a. *Hell Hath No Fury; Innocence Betrayed; Passionate Revenge*
Fugitive Rage (1996), a.k.a. *Caged Fear*
Over the Wire (1996) (as Nicholas Medina)
Masseuse (1996) (as Peter Daniels), a.k.a. *American Masseuse*
Invisible Mom (1997)
Bikini Hoe-Down (1997) (as Roger Collins)
Hybrid (1997)
Invisible Dad (1997)
Little Miss Magic (1997)
Kidwitch (USA: video title)

168 • *Masters of Imagination*

Masseuse 2 (1997) (as Peter Daniels), a.k.a. *Black Stocking Diary*
The Shooter (1997) (as Ed Raymond), a.k.a. *Desert Shooter*
Rapid Assault (1997) (as Sherman Scott)
Maximum Revenge (1997), a.k.a. *Maximum Security*
Night Shade (1997) (as Nicholas Medina)
Mom, Can I Keep Her? (1998)
Mom's Outta Sight (1998) (as Peter Stewart)
Inferno (1998), a.k.a. *Operation Cobra*
Illicit Dreams 2 (1998) (as Roger Collins), a.k.a. *Death & Desire*
Billy Frankenstein (1998)
Dear Santa (1998) (as Peter Stewart), a.k.a. *Secret Santa*
The Kid with X-ray Eyes (1999) (as Sherman Scott)
Invisible Mom II (1999)
Fugitive Mind (1999)
The Prophet (1999), a.k.a. *The Capitol Conspiracy*
Counter Measures (1999), a.k.a. *Crash Dive 2*
Active Stealth (1999)
Scandal: On the Other Side (1999) (as Nick Medina)
Sideshow (2000)
Inviati Speciali (2000)
Submerged (2000)
Critical Mass (2000) (as Ed Raymond)
Emmanuelle 2000 (2001)
Stranded (2001), a.k.a. *Black Horizon; On Eagle's Wings; Space Station*
Air Rage (2001)
Mach 2 (2001)
ACW Wrestling's Wildest Matches! (2001) (as Sherman Scott)
Emmanuelle 2001: Emmanuelle's Sensual Pleasures (2001) (as Nicholas Medina)
Kept (2001) (uncredited), a.k.a. *Playback*
Southern Discomfort: Wrestling on the Indie Circuit (2002)
Venomous (2002) (as Ed Raymond)
13 Erotic Ghosts (2002) (as Nicholas Medina)
Bikini Airways (2003) (as Nicholas Medina)
Final Examination (2003)
Bikini a Go Go (2004) (as Nicholas Medina), a.k.a. *Curse of the Erotic Tiki*
The Bikini Escort Company (2004) (as Nicholas Medina), a.k.a. *The Erotic Escort Company*
Genie in a String Bikini (2004) (as Nicholas Medina)
Haunting Desires (2004) (TV) (as Nicholas Medina)
Teenage Cavegirl (2004) (as Nicholas Medina)
Glass Trap (2005)
The Legend of William Tell (2006)
The Lair (2007) (TV)
Turbulent Skies (2010) TV
American Bandits: Frank and Jesse James (2010)

WRITER

Alien Dead (1980) (screenplay)
Scalps (1983) (screenplay) (story)

Biohazard (1985) (writer)
Armed Response (1986) (story)
Cyclone (1987) (story)
Prison Ship (1987) (story)
Deep Space (1988) (writer)
Bulletproof (1988) (story)
Hollywood Chainsaw Hookers (1988) (screenplay) (as Dr. S. Carver)
The Phantom Empire (1989) (writer)
Bad Girls from Mars (1990) (writer) (as Sherman Scott)
Teenage Exorcist (1991) (story)
Haunting Fear (1991) (writer) (as Sherman Scott)
Soldier's Fortune (1991) (story)
Scream Queen Hot Tub Party (1991) (writer) (as Bill Carson)
Evil Toons (1992) (writer) (as Sherman Scott)
Stepmonster (1993) (story)
Inner Sanctum II (1994) (writer) (as Sherman Scott)
Possessed by the Night (1994) (story)
Jack-O (1995) (story)
Southern Discomfort: Wrestling on the Indie Circuit (2002) (writer)
Thirteen Erotic Ghosts (2002) (written by) (as Sherman Scott)
Bikini Airways (2003) (screenplay) (as Roger Collins)
Bikini a Go Go (2004) (screenplay) (as Sherman Scott)
Tomb of the Werewolf (2004) (writer) (as Sherman Scott)
Genie in a String Bikini (2004) (writer) (as Sherman Scott)
Haunting Desires (2004) (TV) (screenplay) (as Sherman Scott)
Teenage Cavegirl (2004) (writer) (as Sherman Scott)
The Bikini Escort Company (2004) (screenplay) (as Sherman Scott)
Bikini Round-Up (2005) (screenplay) (as Nicholas Medina)
Ghost in a Teeny Bikini (2006) (written by) (as Nicholas Medina)
Bikini Pirates (2006) (written by) (as Nicholas Medina)
The Girl from B.I.K.I.N.I. (2007) (written by) (as Nicholas Medina)
Girl with the Sex-Ray Eyes (2007) (TV) (written by) (as Sherman Scott)
Bewitched Housewives (2007) (TV) (written by) (as Sherman Scott)
"The Lair" (28 episodes, 2007–2009)
Voodoo Dollz (2008) (TV) (written by) (as Nicholas Medina)
Turbulent Skies (2009) (TV)
American Bandits: Frank and Jesse James (2010)

ACTOR

The Brain Leeches (1977)
Alien Dead (1980)
Biohazard (1985)
Armed Response (1986)
Bad Girls from Mars (1990) (as Sherman Scott)
Naked Obsession (1990)
Scream Queen Hot Tub Party (1991) (uncredited)
Double Deception (1993) (TV)
Angel Eyes (1993) (as Sam Newfield)

Inner Sanctum II (1994)
Possessed by the Night (1994)
Mind Twister (1994)
Droid Gunner (1995)
Bikini Drive-In (1995) (as Randy Rocket)
Sorceress (1995)
Hard Bounty (1995)
The Wasp Woman (1995) (TV)
Star Hunter (1995)
Rebellious (1995)
Vampire Vixens from Venus (1995)
Fugitive Rage (1996)
Invisible Mom (1996)
Theater Dark Video Magazine (1996) (TV)
Babe Watch: Forbidden Parody (1996)
Alien Escape (1997)
Inferno (1997)
Just Write (1997)
Bikini Hoe-Down (1997)
Maximum Revenge (1997) (as Bill Carson)
The Prophet (1999) (as Sherman Scott)
Ghost Taxi (1999)
Ride with the Devil (1999
The Voyeur (2000)
Thirteen Erotic Ghosts (2002) (uncredited)
Zombiegeddon (2003)

"When I was writing *Ghost Story* I was very aware that I was at another level from the work I had done before that. I knew something was going to happen, I knew my life was going to change in some way. I was going to make a considerable amount of money. The book seemed so much more powerful than anything I had written."

— *Peter Straub*

The Jazz Man of Horror: Peter Straub

Peter Straub has written within the blanket genre of "speculative fiction" with literacy and critical legitimacy, pleasing fans with a sophisticated mix of style and substance over a career spanning more than three decades. He kicked the door in without trying, with such books as Julia, Ghost Story, The Hellfire Club *and* The Talisman, *the latter co-written with genre giant Stephen King. His prose is intelligent without talking down to the reader, pulling off the most difficult trick of all: keeping his stories both entertaining and exciting.*

Straub continues to explore dark themes both for us and with us, reaching into mystery and suspense as he continues to lead the way. There's always new ground to be broken, which is evident with his second collaboration with King, Black House.

At sixteen, Straub knew he wanted to be a novelist. He obtained a Bachelor of Arts in English at the University of Wisconsin in 1965. He went on to collect his master's degree in contemporary literature at Columbia University.

In 2006, Straub was awarded a Lifetime Achievement Award from the Horror Writers Association. Besides the six Bram Stoker awards, he is the recipient of two International Horror Guild Awards, two World Fantasy Awards, and one British Fantasy Society Award. His website is www.peterstraub.net.

When you wrote the short story "Blue Rose," did you imagine it would blossom into such novels as *The Throat, Koko, Mystery* and *House Without Doors*?

The phrase "Blue Rose" actually came from a book about hypnotism I read when I was about thirteen and used to hypnotize my brothers and a visiting cousin. As in the story, it was used to induce a post-hypnotic suggestion. The actual story came to when I was reading a book called *The Freudian Fallacy*; the author had discovered that the brain waves of those under hypnosis resembled the brain patterns of people having epileptic fits. For some reason, this put Harry Beevers in my mind. I saw the story as a way into *Koko*, but had no idea that two other novels would flow out from it.

What inspired *A Dark Matter*?

I found myself remembering the odd, talkative guru-types who haunted campuses in the mid-sixties, taking advantage of gullible students while living off them. One of these guys told a roomful of students, including me, about seeing a man's hand chopped off in a Tibetan bar. It seemed to mean a lot to him, but I never figured out why or what.

Mr. X himself. Peter Straub on Columbus Avenue in New York City (photograph by Kyle Cassidy, 2009).

You've written a number of mystery and suspense novels. Is it harder to keep a mystery mysterious or a thriller thrilling?

To me, they are very much the same thing. My mystery novels aren't really like the crime novels that anybody has written. When I called my novel *Mystery*, it never occurred to me that everybody in the world would look at that and would say, "Oh that's like *Ghost Story*— he's referring to the genre." I was referring to Mystery with a capital M, the mysterious realm that we sometimes apprehend around us, with a sense of the numinous, with a sense of things unknown. That is something that is not of interest to Rex Stout, Agatha Christie … it is of very little interest to Donald Westlake and Lawrence Block whom I revere and are good friends of mine [and] whose work I enjoy.

What you're asking about, in my terms, is narrative tension. It is very important to me to keep building up a gathering head of steam, so the reader does really wonder, "What will happen next?" There is very little difference between the way that feels in the basically crime context or spooky context. It's the same sense of anxiety, uncertainty, facing the unknown, being puzzled — in short, a layer of suspense.

I would consider you the Jazz Man of Horror. Who are some of the jazz musicians and artists you enjoy?

"The Jazz Man of Horror"— that's very nice, I love it.

The heart in my taste of jazz lies with the people I fell in love with when I first started to hear jazz. My taste has expanded a great deal and I will get to those people in a second.

The core of my taste would sound very palatable for all those who came into the (John) Coltrane era: Paul Desmond, Chet Baker, Stan Getz, Bill Evans, Zoot Sims. From there it folds out to Lester Young, Dexter Gordon — mainly talking about tenor saxophone players. Of course, no jazz fan can't worship Charlie Parker.

When I started listening to jazz, I started listening year by year to the music being made at that time. Then we got up into the late sixties, what Coltrane was doing at that period — and if you weren't attuned to it, it sounded like axe murders. It was overblowing at the top of the horn, no underlying rhythm, no underlying harmony, simply passionate or tortured or ecstatic cries. So there was no place to go from there. You can only go back after that. You can't develop that sound. You can domesticate it, which many thousands of jazz players have done since, domesticate Coltrane and so you can squeeze it back into the harmonic box. What I realized I had to do, I had to go back to the music I had no time for when I was younger.

Once I got into my mid–30s, I started listening backwards. Back to Ben Webster, Vic Dickenson, Duke Ellington, ultimately to Louis Armstrong and Bix Beiderbecke. That is generations of music and if that is what you are interested in, it's a bottomless well.

When you were writing *Ghost Story*, did you imagine it would be as successful as it was? What are your thoughts on the movie?

When I was writing *Ghost Story* I was very aware that I was at another level from the work I had done before that. I knew something was going to happen, I knew my life was going to change in some way. I was going to make a considerable amount of money. The book seemed so much more powerful than anything I had written. So of course, I immediately informed my agent and I immediately informed my publishers to get them worked up. If the book had been a dud, I would have looked like a fool. They all kind of agreed with me, and the end result was that it performed way beyond my expectations. I thought, I might make about a hundred thousand dollars out of the book — to me, that was a vast amount of money. It did infinitely better than that.

When *Ghost Story* was filmed, I was very pleased to think about how the movie might be. It sounded to me like it was full of potential. I loved the cast and the director (John Irving) had done a BBC version of "Tinker Taylor Solider Spy" (from the John Le Carre book), so I knew he could handle difficult complex narratives.

The studio had promised to keep me in touch, promised to let me read the script and offered to let me come to the set and all of that. I should have known something was wrong when the studio rigidly froze me off. They told Larry Cohen the screenwriter not to let me see the screenplay.

I hadn't known what they had done until I went to a screening in New York. I didn't want to admit then how bad I thought it was. It was too disappointing. For me, it was a lost effort.

A lot of people liked that movie and it and it sold another million paperbacks, so it did me a power of good. Every now and then, I run into somebody who is very fond of that movie, and I'm glad they are. If it had been ten percent better, it would have been a hundred percent more effective.

There's been talk of turning *The Talisman* into a mini-series over the years. Any progress?

I have something very interesting news about that.

The Talisman was bought by Universal as a vehicle for Steven Spielberg. Universal bought it because Spielberg told them to. In 1984, Spielberg had tremendous clout. So they bought, gave it to him and he lost interest. It was no longer the sort of thing he felt he wanted to do. He wanted to do more mainstream, more worthy projects. It vanished.

The mini-series idea was floated. Spielberg liked the idea of having a mini-series. He had people in mind to direct it. It went through various revisions and that died.

Five or six years later, Kathleen Kennedy and Spielberg were back to being partners, decided once again to do it as a mini-series for ABC. That sounded like it would work (Mick Garris had written a screenplay and had planned to direct the project). They had a very good script and that died.

Now there's a friend of mine, who is a very, very good writer, I won't name him. But he told me he got a call from his agent who asked if he would be interested in doing a screenplay for a movie of *The Talisman*. My friend said "who would direct it?" And his agent said, "Spielberg." My friend said, "Yeah, I'd like to give that a crack." Who knows, it might happen. I would be very, very pleased to see that particular combination.

The Talisman was re-released shortly before *Black House*. Both novels ended up on the best-sellers list at the same time. Were you surprised that there is still a lot of interest for *The Talisman*?

It was very gratifying to see that. Random House was especially gratified because they had sold a lot more copies of the new version of *The Talisman* then they had expected to, both in hardback and paperback. It was warming and rewarding the book would get a whole new audience all over again. I don't think that happens very much.

I had very mixed feelings about *The Talisman* for a long time. But when I read it in preparation for starting work again with Stephen King on *Black House*, I surprised myself on how much I liked it. I thought it was really, really a nice book.

Did the Internet and electronic media make the collaboration of *Black House* easier?

Yeah, that's right. Though we had one of the first modems in the early '80s. The modems were big machines with telephones on top of them. You had to dial the number, we didn't have hard disks then. The floppys were like 78 records. This was before Windows, so you had to punch in a certain DOS code. Then you could hear your computer make these digesting sounds. Grumble, click, growl. It went on for half an hour while it sent a hundred pages.

When I got the pages from Steve [King] I could see them come onto the empty floppy. Line by line down the page of my monitor. They scrolled by past, but you could still read them.

There were all sorts of glitches in codes. He was using a Wang and I was using an IBM. They had different codes for italics, for bold, all that kind of thing. Even for paragraphing. We had to figure out little symbols to use in place of the ordinary symbols and inform the machine that those symbols were codes: italic, indent, etc.

After I wrote the whole thing, I'd then do a global search and replace for italic, quotation marks. And Steve would do a reverse global replace.

This time around, of course, it was much, much easier. It took seconds to send a hundred pages through the Internet. It is vastly more convenient.

***Black House* tips its hat** to Charles Dickens' *Bleak House* and *The Talisman* is a tribute to Mark Twain's *Tom Sawyer*. Would you consider the series literary horror?

It does reflect that both of its authors have read a hell of a lot of books. We have certain tastes, *Tom Sawyer* meant a lot to both Steve and I when we were kids. *Bleak House* meant to a lot to us in our adulthood. Dickens in general had a big effect on Steve and myself. The title *Black House* is a deliberate reference to *Bleak House*. We sure as hell didn't try to hide it [*laughs*]. We even had one character read *Bleak House* to his best friend.

John Clute (writer and editor of *The Encyclopedias of Fantasy and Science Fiction*,) discovered that the Random House edition of *Black House* contained the same number of pages as the original first edition of *Bleak House*. He was sure it was intentional. Of course, it was a wonderful coincidence.

Koko has been a favorite of yours of your own works. What is it about that novel that you are still fond of?

I'm fond of the fact, while I was writing it I knew I was going somewhere new. I had the strong feeling that my game had moved up to a new level. Nothing can be more rewarding if you write fiction all day long to feel that your work has mysteriously, internally improved. That book was emotionally richer than anything I had written before.

That had something to do with the stories "Blue Rose" and "The Juniper Tree" I wrote en route for *Houses Without Doors*. Those two stories were unlike anything I had written — I wrote them with tremendous concentration and a sense of absolute involvement. I loved them both much while I was doing it. I loved the activity. Those stories are very extreme, they are unpleasant, they force the reader to look at displeasing things very, very close-up. They are also written in such a way, to achieve a kind of transparency. I didn't want any stylistic tricks to fuzzy or interfere with the transaction of the reader on the page.

I had to bring that antiseptic into *Koko*, it is a very demanding aesthetic. I had to revise everything many, many times in order to make the prose really clean and alive.

So that is another reason I like *Koko*, my writing there; although I've always been absurdly proud of my prose style, in that case had finally grew up. I also thought my dialogue had gotten a lot better.

Any works in progress? What is in the future for Peter Straub?

I hope and I must believe there is another novel lurking out there [*laughs*]. [Pulls out little notebook] What I have here in my hand, to quote Joe McCarthy "is not a list of names" but a bunch of notes for a book, with the working title of *Queen of the Night*. (Author's note: These were the initial ideals for the book that would eventually become *Lost Boy Lost Girl*).

I should have begun this a year ago, but I had to do a lot of PR for *Black House*. My collaborator decided to stay at home [*laughs*] and God bless him — I agreed to go out. I did a million book fairs and interviews and stuff like that. That meant I was really too busy, I'm not one of those writers who can write where he is. I need boredom, I need stillness, I need some kind of routine for my imagination to wake up.

Then September 11th slowed me down a great deal. It was very, very depressing. It was in the city that I lived in. It had been very seriously wounded. And for a long time that wound was open. I couldn't forget the fact that three miles from me there was a big, big pile of corpses. This is the way horror writers think. The smell of dead bodies was in the air down there.

I emerged from that, because I had to. I had to write some introductions. That helped me get back into the habit of stringing sentences together. It was a difficult thing. If you haven't done it for a while it is daunting. To make sentences link up, that don't fall over themselves and actually say something. I wrote a very long introduction for a Larry Block book — which was about twenty pages. Then I wrote an introduction for *The Stepford Wives* (by Ira Levin).

My friend Bradford Morrow, the editor of the literary journal called "Conjunctions" (issue #39) asked me to guest edit an issue. He wanted me to get his favorite writers to write horror stories — an idea I felt was really repulsive. So I suggested that we do something a lot more interesting — bring together under one roof those writers who seemed to me had begun to erase the boundaries in the genre-world. These writers who have since created really noteworthy, memorable books but whose names aren't known to the general public. This is a very nice Trojan Horse for everyone involved. All the writers who I talked to, who I approached were immediately enthusiastic about it. What I'm doing is writing my story at the moment. I'm about halfway through my story for this issue. That "Conjunctions" issue should come out in the fall and is going to be called "The New Fabulous." The effect when we're done is a really good anthology, with these writers who are the forefront of post-genre writing.

When that is done, I will at last start seriously to begin on that novel that I carry around in a notebook now. The novel in my pocket [*laughs*].

Last question, any advice for beginning writers?

I think beginning writers should read their heads off. I think they should read everything they can get. I think they should read the best books they can get. The worst thing any beginning horror writer can do, is to read only horror. Especially horror written by people of their generation — and mistake those people for "it." By "it" I mean achieved writing — everyone who you were forced to read in school and hated. You should go back and look at: (F. Scott) Fitzgerald, (Ernest) Hemingway, (John) Steinbeck, Charles Dickens, Wilkie Collins, George Eliot, the Brontes, John Updike, Phillip Roth, (Leo) Tolstoy, (Marcel) Proust and (Feodor) Dostoyevsky — that is the kind of people you should be reading if you want to write. You don't want to invent the wheel, you don't want to think of the world as flat. You want writing with some dimension in it and then while your doing that, you just have to write, write and write. You have to write out all the bad stuff. Every writer has within them a mountain of trash and you have to excrete that stuff before you can get to the good stuff. The reason you have to do it is you have to discover in that process who you are.

It took me a long time to find out what I was good at. I wouldn't have believed it when I started. I thought what I would be good at was John Ashbury post-narrative contemporary novels. I discovered what I was good at was plot, narrative, tension, and a certain subset of feelings — I didn't even want that. When I discovered I was good at it, I really wanted to expand that and develop it. I think that is one of the essential tasks of young writers, to discover their real voice and their real material. It's a hard wrestle, but it's supposed to be hard.

Writing fiction is impossible — you are trying to create a completely made-up world that can replace the real world. It has to be seamless, every detail has to have vitality in it, all the verbs have sizzle in them. When you put the perfect book down on a table, it would float on a little electrical charge of air two or three inches above the table, it would sit there humming. I keep on trying to write that book — but I can't. That is the ultimate goal.

Books by Peter Straub

NOVELS

Marriages (1973)
Under Venus (1985)
Julia (1975)
If You Could See Me Now (1977)
Ghost Story (1979)
Shadowland (1980)
Floating Dragon (1983)
The Talisman, with Stephen King (1984)
Koko (1988)
Mystery (1990)
The Throat (1993)
The Hellfire Club (1996)
Mr. X (1999)
Black House, with Stephen King (2001)
Lost Boy Lost Girl (2004)
In The Night Room (2004)
A Dark Matter (2010)

Novellas Published in Limited Editions

The General's Wife (1982)
Mrs. God (1991)
Blue Rose (1995)
Pork Pie Hat (1999)

Collections

Wild Animals (*Julia, If You Could See Me Now, Under Venus*) (1984)
Houses Without Doors (1990)
Magic Terror (2000)
A Little Blue Book Of Rose Stories (2004)
5 Stories (2007)

Poetry

My Life in Pictures (1974)
Ishmael (1972)
Open Air (1972)
Lesson Park & Belsize Square (1984)
The Devil's Wine, edited by Tom Piccirilli (2004)

Edited by Peter Straub

Peter Straub's Ghosts (1995)
Conjunctions #39: The New Wave Fabulists (2002)
H.P. Lovecraft: Weird Tales (2004), edited, notes and chronology by Peter Straub
American Fantastic Tales: Terror and The Uncanny from Poe to the Pulps (2009)
American Fantastic Tales: Terror and The Uncanny from the 1940s Until Now (2009)

Awards

1989 World Fantasy Award
Best Novel, for *Koko*
1993 Bram Stoker Award
Best Novel, for *The Throat*
1993 World Fantasy Award
Best Novella, for "The Ghost Village"
1994 British Fantasy Award
Best Novel, for *Floating Dragon*
1998 Bram Stoker Award
Long Fiction for "Mr. Clubb and Mr. Cuff"
1998 International Horror Guild Award
Best Long Form, for "Mr. Clubb and Mr. Cuff"
1999 Bram Stoker Award
Best Novel, for *Mr. X*

2000 Bram Stoker Award
Fiction Collection, for *Magic Terror*
2003 International Horror Guild Award
Best Novel, for *Lost Boy Lost Girl*
2003 Bram Stoker Award
Best Novel, for *Lost Boy Lost Girl*
2007 Bram Stoker Award
Superior Achievement in a Collection, for *5 Stories*

Afterword
by Gregory Lamberson

Merriam-Webster defines imagination, in part, as "a creation of the mind; *especially*: an idealized or poetic creation."

Everyone who reads this book possesses imagination; it's likely that every living person, regardless of their state of mind, possesses imagination. Imagination is one of the key ingredients of humanity. A child dreaming of one day journeying to the stars has imagination. So does a working mother looking forward to clocking out so she can go home. A man fantasizing about his dream date probably uses his imagination for recreational purposes. And an incarcerated felon awaiting his stab at parole no doubt uses his imagination to hang onto his sanity.

Imagination is not restricted to creators in the various fields of arts and entertainment, but those creators have managed to harness their imaginative impulses and channel them in a way that liberates them. As a friend once said to me, "Writers don't write because they want to, they write because they *have* to."

My friend was right. Writers, musicians, painters and filmmakers follow their paths — often at great personal sacrifice, occasionally with rewards — because they need a creative outlet. Referring to the title of this book, they have *mastered* their imagination ... or their imaginations have mastered *them*.

As a novelist and film director, I like the range of "imagineers" selected for this book: authors, filmmakers and actors from the spectrum of science fiction, fantasy and horror. I grew up reading Ray Bradbury. William F. Nolan was my pen pal when I was in junior high school. John Carpenter legitimized horror films among my classroom peers. Peter Straub set my imagination on fire with *Ghost Story* in high school. Nate Kenyon and I comforted each other after we both lost a Bram Stoker Award to Stephen King. My friend Joe McKinney wrote one of my favorite zombie novels. I once mailed some S&M

paraphernalia to someone featured in this book because after he purchased it he feared embarrassment if his bags were examined at the airport. How's *that* for imagination?

But I like that Michael McCarty has not discriminated against the world of low-budget filmmaking in this survey of creative forces, which is often the tendency among critics, even genre critics. There's Fred Olen Ray, auteur of more B movies than I can count, and Linnea Quigley, who rose to fame dancing naked on a gravestone in *Return of the Living Dead,* sharing the Table of Contents with acclaimed author Thomas Ligotti. Actors require imagination just as much as writers do; it's one of their primary tools. If they don't believe what they're saying in a film, how can *we*? And these days, when so many actors perform their craft in front of a green screen, they need more imagination than ever.

If you're like me, you read books like this out of order, favoring those chapters devoted to your heroes and friends. I hope you'll continue to follow my lead and return to those sections profiling creators who are less known to you; there are some real gems here.

And now I leave you with this question: Is it possible to be the master of your imagination *and* the master of your domain?

Think about it!

Back in black, Gregory Lamberson (photograph by Richard Wicka, 2006).

About the Author

MICHAEL MCCARTY has been a professional writer since 1983 and is the author of numerous books of fiction and nonfiction, as well as hundreds of articles, short stories, and poems. In 2009 he was named as a finalist, along with collaborator Mark McLaughlin, in two different Bram Stoker Award categories: Best First Novel of 2008 for *Monster Behind the Wheel* (Corrosion Press/ Delirium Books), and Best Poetry Collection of 2008 for *Attack of the Two-Headed Poetry Monster* (Skullvines Press). He received the 2008 David R. Collins' Literary Achievement Award from the Midwest Writing Center. In 2005, he was a Bram Stoker Award finalist in the nonfiction category for *More Giants of the Genre*.

Michael lives in Rock Island, Illinois with his wife Cindy and pet rabbit Latte, and is a former stand-up comedian, musician and managing editor of a music magazine.

photo by Ray Congrove

His websites include http:// www.goodreads.com/michaelmccarty, www.myspace.com/ monsterbook, www.myspace.com/ottochurch, www.myspace.com/monsterpoetrybook, and Michael McCarty – Davenport, Iowa at Facebook.

He can be contacted at:
>Mike McCarty
>P.O. Box 4441
>Rock Island, IL 61201
>mikelmccarty@hotmail.com